MAN AND WOMAN

AND CHILD

BOOKS BY HAROLD W. PERCIVAL

THINKING AND DESTINY
Libr. of Congress 47-1811
ISBN: 0-911650-09-1 (one vol. deluxe hardcover)
ISBN: 0-911650-06-7 (one vol. quality softcover)

MASONRY AND ITS SYMBOLS
In the Light of Thinking and Destiny
Libr. of Congress 52-2237
ISBN: 0-911650-07-5

MAN AND WOMAN AND CHILD
Libr. of Congress 52-6126
ISBN: 0-911650-08-3

DEMOCRACY IS SELF-GOVERNMENT
Libr. of Congress 52-30629
ISBN: 0-911650-10-5

Available from your local bookstore, or from:

The Word Foundation, Inc.
P.O. Box 17510
Rochester, NY 14617
www.thewordfoundation.org

MAN AND WOMAN AND CHILD

AND CHILD

by Harold W. Percival

Inquiries Welcome

The Word Foundation, Inc.
P.O. Box 17510
Rochester, NY 14617
www.thewordfoundation.org

First Edition, 1951
Second Edition, 1979
Third Edition, 1992

ISBN: 0-911650-08-3

Printed in U.S.A.
by Taylor Publishing Company

DEDICATED

WITH LOVE

TO THE

CONSCIOUS SELF

IN

EVERY

HUMAN BODY

CONTENTS

PART V

THE HUMAN BEING
FROM ADAM TO JESUS

PREFACE

This book was written with *Thinking and Destiny* as a background, published four years ago. That work is somewhat in the nature of a textbook. It is concerned with the great Cosmos in its entirety and in all its parts, even to the minutest constituents. The book states the One Reality to be: *CONSCIOUSNESS ABSOLUTE.* It shows that the Universe is governed intelligently; that Justice reigns throughout; that Man is not a plaything of accident or chance but that, on the contrary, his Destiny has been, and is being, made by his own thinking and doing; and—How all this came about.

From the information furnished in *Thinking and Destiny* there has been selected for special treatment in *Man and Woman—and Child*, the part played by the human:—How in the dim past, he lived in what in the Scriptures is called "Paradise" or the "Garden of Eden," in a sexless body; and how it came to pass that he "fell" from his high estate and thereafter lived in the condition of man and woman—out of which he must and in time will, arise and free himself by his own efforts, to enter upon the Great Path to *Conscious Immortality*—as outlined in pages to follow.

M.E. JUTTE, M.D.
New York, 1951

FOREWORD

This book is to tell the men and women who are weary of thinking with "The Way of the World," weary of turning the continuous treadmill of human life and death and rebirth, that there is a better way—The Great Way to The Realm of Bliss with Peace and Power in Perpetuity. But it is not an easy way. The Great Way begins with the understanding of yourself.

The name given the body you inhabit is not *you*. You do not know *who* you are or *what* you are, awake or asleep. The intellectual understanding of *what* you are, in the mortal coils of blood and nerves in which you are entangled, will allow you to engage in the process of thinking to identify and distinguish yourself as the conscious self in, and as different from the body in which *you* are hidden. The process of thinking continues with the practice of self-control, and it progresses gradually through rebuildings and transformations of the physical mortal body in which you dwell, to actually live in a physical body of immortal life—with gracious beauty and conscious power transcending human thought.

You, as the conscious "I" or self in the body—that which is absent from the body during sleep—can do this when you become conscious of *what* you are, and where and how and why you are incarcerated in the physical body in which you are.

These assertions are not based on fanciful hopes. They are substantiated by the anatomical, physiological, biological and psychological evidences given herein which you can, if you will, examine, consider and judge; and, then do what you think best.

H. W. P.

PART I

Man and Woman, and Child

One hundred years should be the normal life of man and of woman, approximately divided into four periods or stages in the journey through life. First, youth, which is the stage for education and the learning of self-control; second, maturity, as the stage for learning of human relations; third, accomplishment, as the stage for service to larger interests; and, last, balance, as the stage or period during which one can comprehend and may perform the purifying rites which one ordinarily passes through in the after-death states, or perhaps even begin the regeneration of the physical body.

The four stages are not equally divided as to time; they are developed by one's attitude of mind, and by thinking. Sports, amusements, or social requirements and enjoyments will be compatible with one's age, associations and personal selection. The four stages are not to be considered as stern necessity but as the chosen duties, in which one performs what he chooses and wills.

The first stage begins when the infant body comes into this world; it is only an animal body; but it is different from other animal bodies; it is the most helpless of all animals; it cannot walk or do anything for itself. To continue to live, it must be nursed and coddled and trained to eat and to walk and to talk and repeat what it is told; it does not ask questions. Then, out of the darkness of infancy, comes the dawn of childhood. When the child begins to ask questions, it is evidence that a conscious something, a self, has come into the body, and it is then a human being.

The questioning conscious self makes the difference and distinguishes it from the animal. This is the period of childhood. Then its real education should begin. The parents do not usually know that they are not the parents of the conscious something, the self, which has taken residence in their child; nor do they know that it has an individual ancestry of character. The individual conscious self in the child is immortal; the corporeal body it is in, is subject to death. With the growth of body there will be, there must be, a contest between the conscious self and the animal body, to decide which shall rule.

Therefore, if the conscious self does not learn of its immortality during childhood, it is not probable that it will learn during or after adolescence; then the body-mind will make the conscious self believe it is the body, and will prevent it from identifying itself within the body and from becoming consciously immortal. That is what has happened, and happens, to practically every human being born into this world. But it need not be so, for when the conscious something in the young child—as occurs almost invariably—begins to ask its mother, what it is and where it came from, it should be told that a physical body was necessary to enable it to come into this physical world, and so father and mother provided the physical body in which it is. By asking the conscious something questions about itself, its thinking will be centered on itself instead of on its body, and thus be turned into the proper channels. But if it thinks more about its body than it does about itself, then it will come to identify itself with and as the physical body. The parents should carefully note the attitudes, attractions and repulsions of the child; its generosity or selfishness; its questions and its answers to questions. Thus, the character which is latent in the child can be observed. Then it can be taught to control the bad and to educate, draw out and develop the good in itself. Among the multitude of children that come into the world there are at least a few with whom this is possible, and of the few there should be one who would make the conscious connection with its greater Self. When a child is so educated, it will be prepared to take its courses in such schools as will qualify it for the chosen field of work in the world.

The second stage, maturity, is to be marked by the qualifying characteristics of independence and responsibility. One's work in the world will serve this purpose. During development, youth must outgrow the need for nursing and dependence on its parents by calling into activity and using its own potential resources to provide and make a place for itself in the community. The doing of this develops responsibility. To be responsible means that one is trustworthy; that he will make good his promises and will fulfill the obligations of all his undertakings.

The third stage should be the period of accomplishment, for service of whatever kind. The education of youth and the experience and learning of human relations should be the ripened maturity that can best serve the community or State in the position or capacity for which one is best fitted.

The fourth and final stage of the human being should be the period for balance when retired from active work, for the contemplation of oneself. It should be in review of one's own past thoughts and acts in relation to the future. One's thoughts and deeds can then be examined and impartially judged while in life, by thinking, instead of waiting until and when, in the after-death states, one must judge them in his Hall of Judgment by the Conscious Light. There, without the physical body, one cannot do any new thinking; he can only think over what he has thought and done while alive in the physical body. While living, each one can intelligently think over and prepare oneself for the next life on earth. One might even discover his conscious self in the body, and balance his thoughts so completely as to attempt to regenerate his physical body for an everlasting life.

The foregoing outline of the normal four stages is what they can be or may be if the human understands that he is not a mere puppet who by circumstance or position is made to do what the senses would move him to do. If one is to determine what he will or will not do, he will not allow himself to act as if he were, by the senses, pulled or impelled to act. When he finds or determines what his purpose in the world is, he will thereafter work for that purpose, and all other acts or enjoyments will be incidental to this purpose.

In the morning of life, the conscious self comes into the body and wakens in the dawn of unfolding childhood. Gradually the conscious self in the child becomes aware of sights and sounds and tastes and smells in the strange world in which it finds itself. Slowly it apprehends the meaning of the word-sounds spoken. And the conscious self learns to speak.

With the growth of children there is a mystery, a strange attraction, between boy and girl. Through the years, the mystery is not solved; it continues. The maid sees weakness with his strength; the youth sees ugliness with her beauty. As man and woman, they should learn that the way through life is made up of light and shade, of such opposites as pain and pleasure, bitter and sweet, each succeeding another, as day succeeds night or as peace follows war. And, like the opening of the world to youth, by experience and thinking, man and woman should learn that the causes of unfoldment of the phenomena of the world are not to be found or solved in the world outside themselves, but in the world within; that within each breast are the opposites, pain and pleasure, sorrow and joy, war and peace, which, though unseen, are rooted in the

4

human heart; and that, by branching outwardly by thought and act, they bear their fruits as vices or virtues or curses or blessings in the outer world at large. When one really seeks the self within, he will have cessation of warring and troubling, and find peace—even in this world—the peace beyond the reach of death.

The mystery and problem of men and women are the personal affairs of every man and of every woman. But hardly anybody seriously considers the matter until he is shocked and faced by some fact of life or of death. Then that one is made conscious of the mystery, the problem concerning birth or health or wealth or honor or death or life.

One's physical body is the testing-ground, the means and the instrument by and through which all trials and tests can be made; and what is thought and done will be the evidence and proof and the demonstration of what has or has not been accomplished.

It will now be well to announce the newcomers, to look at their adventures and experiences in their lives, and to consider for the few who *will* to conquer death by regenerating their physical bodies—how to be the "forerunners" who will show the Way to the Kingdom of Heaven or Kingdom of God—The Realm of Permanence—which pervades this world of change, but which cannot be seen by mortal eyes.

Here they come: baby boys and baby girls! hundreds of them, every hour of the day and of the night; out of the invisible into the visible, out of the darkness into the light, with a gasp and a cry—they come; and not only for thousands but for millions of years they have been coming. In frozen north and torrid zone and temperate climes they come. On blistering desert and in sunless jungle, on mountain and in valley, on ocean and in cave, into crowded slums and on desolate coasts, in palace and in hut they come. They come as white or yellow or red or black, and as intermixtures of these. They come into races and nations and families and tribes, and they may be made to live in any part of the earth.

Their coming brings happiness and pain and joy and vexation, and they are received with anxiety and with great acclaim. They are fostered with love and with tender care, and are treated with indifference and gross neglect. They are reared in atmospheres of health and of disease, of refinement and indecency, of wealth and poverty, and they are brought up in virtue and in vice.

They come from man and woman and they develop into men and women. Everybody knows that. True, but that is only one of the facts concerned with the coming of baby boys and baby girls. And when the passengers land from a ship that has just come into port and the question is asked: What are they and where did they come from?, it is also valid to answer: They are men and women and they came from the ship. But that does not really answer the question. Boys and girls do not know why they came or how they came or when they came into the world, nor do men and women know why or how or when they came into or will leave the world. Because nobody remembers, and because of the constant coming of baby boys and baby girls, their coming causes no wonder; it is a common fact. But suppose nobody desired marriage and that all people just lived on and on and did not die; that, too, would be a common fact, and there would be no wonder about it. Then, if into the childless, deathless world there should come a baby boy and a baby girl: what a wonder there would be! Indeed, that would be wonderful. Never had there been such happening before. Then everybody would wonder, and wonder would lead to thinking. And thinking would give a new start to feeling-and-desire. Then again would come the steady stream of baby boys and baby girls. So the gates of birth and death would open and would be kept open in the world. Then the wonder would be that one should wonder, because that would be the natural course of events, even as it is today.

Everybody thinks as everybody does. To think or to do otherwise is against the rule and run of things. People merely see and hear and perhaps they believe, but they never understand. They do not know the mystery of birth.

Why do babies come as they do? How do the two microscopic specks merge and change from an embryo into an infant, and what makes the helpless little creature grow and develop into a man or a woman? What causes one to be a man and the other to be a woman? One does not know.

The baby and the man and woman bodies are machines— mysterious mechanisms. They are the most wonderfully constituted, the most delicately adjusted, and the most intricately complicated mechanisms in the world. The human machine makes all other machines that are made, and it is the machine without which no other machine can be made or operated. But who knows *who* it is or *what* it is that makes and operates the human machine?

The human machine is a living machine and it needs food for its growth and exercise for its organic development. Unlike inanimate machines, the human machine is the grower and the harvester of its food, which comes from the mineral and vegetable and animal kingdoms, and from the water, the air and the sunlight. Of course, everybody knows that, too. Very well, but who knows the mystery of it, which is akin to the mystery of the baby? What is it in the seed or the soil that makes the sugarbeet and the burning pepper, the almost tasteless potato or cabbage, the strong garlic, and what makes the sweet and sour fruits—all growing from the same kind of soil? What is it in the seed that combines the constituents of earth, water, air and light into vegetables and fruits? What causes the organs in the body to secrete as they do, and with their secretions to separate foods into their constituents, and to compound and transform these into blood and flesh and brain and bone and sinew and skin and hair and tooth and nail and germ cell? What fashions these materials and holds them always in the same order and form; what molds the features and gives them color and shade; and what gives grace or awkwardness to the movements of the human machine, with a distinctiveness of its own from every other machine? Uncounted thousands of tons of foodstuffs are consumed every day by the man and woman machines, and every day as many tons are returned to the earth, the water and the air. In this way is kept up a circulation and a balance of the elements through and by means of the man and woman machines. These serve as so many clearing houses for the exchanges carried on between nature and the human machine. The answer to such questions is that ultimately all this is due to the Conscious Light in nature.

Now when the baby boy or baby girl arrived, it could not see or hear or taste or smell. These special senses were in the baby, but the organs had not sufficiently developed so that the senses could be adjusted to the organs and trained to use them. At first the baby could not even crawl. It was the most helpless of all the little animals that come into the world. It could only cry and coo and nurse and wiggle. Later, after it had been trained to see and to hear and it could sit up and stand, it was trained in the venturesome performance of walking. When the baby could toddle around without support it was said to be able to walk, and to walk was indeed an astonishing achievement for a baby. About this time it learned to pronounce and to repeat a few words, and it was supposed to be able to talk. While attaining to these accomplishments, the senses of sight, hearing, taste and smell were being adjusted to their respective nerves, and these nerves were being fitted and attuned to their respective organs: the eye, the ear, the tongue, and the nose. And then the senses and nerves and organs were so coordinated and related to each other that they worked together as one organized mechanism. All these processes in the life of the baby were to develop it into a living and automatically working machine. Long before this, the living machine had been given a name, and it learned to answer to some such name as John or Mary.

You do not remember any of these undertakings and events in your life, as a baby. Why? Because *you* were not the baby; *you* were not in the baby, or at least, not enough of *you* was in the baby body or in touch with the senses to remember the developments and exploits of the baby. It would indeed be disquieting for you to remember all the things that the baby, which was being prepared for you, either did or had done for it to make it ready for you to come into it and to live in it.

Then, one day, an extraordinary and very important event took place. Around and into the living baby named John or Mary, there came a conscious something that was conscious of *itself*, conscious as being *not* John or Mary. But when that conscious something was in John or Mary it was unable to identify itself as being distinct, and as *not* John or *not* Mary. It was not conscious of where it came from, or where it was, or how it got wherever it then happened to be. That is the way it was when *you*, as a conscious self had come into the body you inhabit.

As a little John or Mary body the baby had responded to the impressions it had received as an automatic machine would respond, without being conscious of what was happening. The baby was still a machine, but a machine plus the "something" that had come into it. Just what the something was, certainly the something did not know. It was conscious of itself, but it could not understand what itself was; it could not explain itself to itself. It was bewildered. It was also conscious of the body in which it lived and moved and felt, but it could not definitely identify itself, so as to say: I am this, myself, and the body which I feel is something *in* which I am. The conscious something *then* feels itself to be the conscious "I" in the John or in the Mary body, just as you now think of and feel the clothes you wear to be different from the body, and not the body which wears the clothes. You were then sure you were *not* the body.

You were in a dreadful plight! Therefore, after wondering about the matter a long while, the conscious something asked the mother questions such as these: Who am I? What am I? Where am I? Where did I come from? How did I get here? What do such questions mean? They mean that the conscious something has a past! Nearly every conscious something which comes into the baby is sure to ask such questions of the mother as soon as it gets over its first daze from coming in, and is able to ask questions. Of course these were puzzling questions, and disconcerting to the mother, because she could not answer them. She made some answer which did not satisfy. The same or similar questions have been asked by the conscious something in nearly every boy and girl that has come into the world. The mother was at one time in the same predicament in which the "I," the *you* was then. But she had forgotten that what was then happening to you, in John or in Mary, was practically the same that had happened to herself when she came into her body. And so she gave you the same or similar answers to your questions as those which she had received from the parents of her body. She told you that the little body in which you then were, was *you*; that your name was John or that it was Mary; that you were her little boy, or her little girl; that you came from heaven, or some other place of which she knew nothing but of which she had been told; and, that the stork, or the doctor, had brought you. Her intention and her answers were given to satisfy the *you*, in the John or the Mary, and with the hope that they would stop your questioning. But about the mystery of conception, gestation and birth, she knew little more than you did. And she knew still less than you did at that time about the greater mystery of the conscious something which was not her baby but which was asking, through the child body, the questions which she herself had asked and had long ago forgotten.

The baby had lived without regard to past or future. The John or Mary did not distinguish between day and night. But now that the "I," *you*, had come into it, it was no longer a baby, it was a child, and you began to live in the time-world, to be conscious of day and of night, and to expect a tomorrow. How long a day seemed! And how many strange happenings there could be in a day! Sometimes you were among many people and they praised or petted you, or made fun with you, or you were scolded. They treated you as something different. You were a stranger in a strange land. And you—sometimes—felt lonesome and alone. Eventually, you found that it was useless to ask questions about yourself; but you wanted to learn something about the strange world into which you had come, and you asked about the things you saw. You got used to answer to the name of John or Mary. And though you knew you were not, still, you answered to that name. Later, you became restless, and would seek activity; to do, to do, just to keep doing something, anything at all.

To the boy and girl, play is important; it is a serious matter. But to the man and woman it is merely the nonsense of a "child's play." The man and the woman do not understand that the little fellow, who says he is the conqueror, can by the mere waving of his wooden sword and saying "die!" slay armies of tin soldiers; that the dauntless knight bestride his spirited broomstick-horse tramples down a terrible dragon garden-hose and lets it spout forth fire and steam while it dies under the fearless thrusts of his drumstick-spear; that bits of string and a few sticks suffice to erect and suspend over a little puddle from shore to shore a bridge; that with a few cards or blocks he builds up a cloud-piercing, sky-scraping edifice; that on the seashore the brave defender of his country raises up great sand castles and cities, protected by a navy of cockleshells and armies of pebbles and against which the winds and tides dare not prevail; that with buttons for money and a handful of cotton or corn the tiny merchant prince buys or sells huge harvests, and ships great cargos of fabrics and foodstuffs to foreign shores in his grand fleet of paper boats sailing the high seas—on a little water, in his mother's dishpan.

The accomplishments of the girl are scarcely less astonishing than the great deeds of the boy. In a few minutes she easily raises a large family, teaches the boys and girls their respective duties, marries them off, and raises another lot. The next moment she finds a further outlet for her energy by ordering the instant building of a castle, attending to its extraordinary furnishings and entertaining friends or the entire countryside. Strange objects which she fabricates out of anything at hand and calls her babies and children, have equal or greater values than expensive dolls. With ribbons or rags she creates or adorns men and women or such other objects as may suit her fancy. An attic with its rubbish she transforms into a palace and receives royalty; or she gives a grand fete, in any corner of her room. Then she may suddenly leave to keep an appointment in the garden with no particular person. There, fairy visitors may transport her into fairy palaces or show her the wonders of fairyland. One of her privileges is, when she chooses, to create anything she pleases out of nothing at all.

These performances may be not merely for the benefit of the solitary performer. Other girls and boys may be assigned to parts and may help to perform whatever happens. Indeed, the wonder-working of one can be changed into whatever the other suggests, and every one of the party sees and understands what is being done by the others. They are all consciously living in the boy-and-girl world. Everything is strange or nothing is strange. Anything may happen. Their world is the world of make-believe.

The world of make-believe! How did the boy and the girl enter it? They entered it and they helped to maintain it by contacting the senses of sight and sound and taste and smell, and then by seeing and hearing and tasting and smelling. At about the time of one's first memory of the world, the "conscious something" came into the boy or into the girl. It could not see or hear nor could it taste or smell, but gradually it got into gear with those senses of the body and it learned to use them. Then it began to dream, and found that it was in a strange world, and it did not know what to do about it. The little animal body in which it found itself had been taught to articulate its breathing into word-sounds. These words were arranged into the parts of speech used by human beings to represent the things and happenings of the strange world in which it was, so that the people in the world could speak to each other about what they saw and heard, and so that they could describe these things to each other and tell what they thought about anything.

The boy and girl had learned to pronounce these words, just as a parrot does. But that in the boy or in the girl which was the "something" conscious of itself, learned what the word meant and it knew what it was talking about. Well, about the time the boy or girl could do this, the conscious something in him or in her began to think and to ask questions about itself, and about the body, and the world in which it found itself. Of course it could not find out what it was, because the senses of the body could tell it of the body only; it was bewildered; it had lost the memory of who or what it was, as men or women have periods of amnesia when they lose their power of speech or forget their identity. Then there was no one who could tell it anything about itself, because the something "conscious of itself" in every man or woman had long ago forgotten. There were no words that the conscious something could use to tell about itself, even if it were free enough to do so; words meant something about the body and about the world around it. And the more it saw and heard the less it was able to think about itself; and, on the other hand, the more it thought about itself the less it knew about its body and about the world.

It tried to do two kinds of thinking. One kind was about itself, and the other was about the body in which it was and about the people and the world around it. It could not reconcile itself with its body and its surroundings, and it could not clearly distinguish itself from these. It was in an unhappy and confused state, like trying to be itself and not itself at the same time, and not understanding either of the things it was trying to be. Therefore, it could not completely be itself or entirely be the body. It could not be completely itself because of the portion of itself which had become geared into the body by the senses of the body, and it could not think and live in the man and woman world because the organs of the body in which it was were not sufficiently developed so that it could think and live itself into the patterns of the man and woman world. So there was nothing else for it to do than to be in the boy and girl world, the world of make-believe.

Why is the boy and girl world the world of make-believe? Because everything in it is real and nothing is real. Everything in the world seems real to the senses of the body when the "conscious something" in the body identifies itself with the senses, and nothing is real to that conscious something when it is conscious of itself as being *not* of the body or of the senses of the body. The body is not conscious of itself as a body, the senses are not conscious of themselves as senses, and they are not conscious of the body at all. The senses are instruments, and the body is an instrument or a machine, through which the senses are used as instruments. These are not conscious of themselves in any way, and the conscious something which uses them as instruments is not conscious of them or of the objects of the world when it is in deep sleep. In deep sleep the "conscious something" is out of touch with the body and its senses and, therefore, it is not conscious of them or of the body or of the world. Then the body and its senses cannot in any way communicate with the conscious something. While the body sleeps the conscious something retires to a part of itself which is not in gear with the body. When the conscious something returns and is again in touch with the body, it is stricken with forgetfulness of itself. It is again befuddled by the senses with the seeing and the hearing of things and with the name of the body which it must assume. It is conscious of itself as real and of things as unreal when it thinks of itself; and it is conscious

14

of the things of the world as real when it thinks through the senses.

Before the conscious something is entirely shut in by the senses of the body it is in a paradoxical situation. It is conscious of itself as something which is not the body, but it cannot distinguish its body as not itself. It is conscious that all things are possible for it, as the conscious something; and it is conscious of being limited in all things by its body. There is confidence in everything, and there is no assurance of the permanence of anything. Anything may in a moment be created, and in a flash it may be made to disappear or be changed into some other thing, according to the wish. A sawhorse may be used as a prancing steed and a soapbox as a golden chariot, and they may at the same time be the sawhorse and the soapbox, or they may be any other things, or nothing at all, by demanding them so to be or not to be. Then things are not, by supposing them not to be; and things that are not are, by fancying them to be. Now that is simple—and too ridiculous to believe! Well, the conscious something in the body which is conscious of itself and of the body, and which by thinking is conscious that it is not the body, and also by thinking makes itself believe it is the body, learns to follow where the body senses lead, and as its fancy pleases. That is why the conscious something in the boy and in the girl makes the world of make-believe and lives in it—and of which men and women are almost, if not quite, unconscious.

The conscious something knows it is not the body with a name because: it is conscious that it is conscious; it is not conscious that the body is conscious as part of itself; it is not conscious as part of the body; therefore it, as the conscious something, is separate and distinct from the body in which it is, and it is not the name to which it answers. The conscious something does not reason about this. To it the facts are self-evident—that is enough.

But the conscious something in the boy or girl becomes observant; it compares and sometimes reasons about what it sees and hears. If not instructed it will of itself notice that there are certain usages in speech and behavior for different people in the particular relation they bear to each other, between parents, children, domestics, guests, and in social gatherings. The conscious something in the child notices much more than the child is given credit for. It sees that everybody says and does what everybody else says and does, each in his place and in his relation to the others. Everybody appears to imitate others. Therefore, when boys and girls assume their parts and play them, these are to them as important and as real as are the parts which men and women play. They see the parts as a game, the game of make-believe.

Boys and girls will carry on their performances wherever they happen to be. They are not, in this modern age, disturbed by the presence of their elders. When they are questioned concerning their "absurd" or "nonsensical" play, they readily explain. But they feel hurt or unjustly treated when what they say or do is ridiculed. And they often feel pity for men and women who are unable to understand.

When the conscious something has learned to play the part of the body and of the name it has assumed, it becomes conscious that it can as well choose any other name for the body of John or Mary and play the part taken. It hears the names of people, of animals and of objects mentioned by men and women, and it takes and plays the part of the person, animal or object which strikes its fancy and which it chooses to play. Thus the conscious something learns the art of imitation and also the art of masquerade. It is just as natural and as easy for it to assume the name and play the part of father, mother, soldier, vocation, trade or animal, as it is to answer to the name and play the part of John or Mary. It inherently knows that in reality it is not the body named John or Mary any more than it is any other body with a name. Therefore it may just as well call the body in which it is by any other name and play that part.

What is done by the boy and girl about the questions that puzzle and disturb them? Nothing. No answers satisfy them. And there is nothing that can be done about it. So they learn to take for granted things as they seem to be. Each new thing is at first wonderful and in a little while it is just commonplace.

Little John with his penny pistol may break into any bank, right on the street or in his own backyard, and command: "Stick 'em up, ev'ry bod'ee!" Of course, at the sound of that awful voice and before that dreadful gun, everybody obeys and trembles. Then the fearless robber gathers up and carries off the plunder.

John kidnaps Mary and both hide and are thrilled while other boys and girls are excitedly running around, searching and offering rewards for the return of the darling child. Then there is great joy when the heartless kidnapper receives the ransom, paid in newspaper bills, and precious little Mary is recovered.

The men and women do not enjoy these "pranks," nor can they understand them, because long ago they left the boy and girl world and they are not now conscious of it, although they see the boy and girl seriously carrying on right there before them.

Story books for the boy and girl make deeper impressions on them than the popular books make on man and woman. Let the man or woman who has read "Robinson Crusoe" or "The Swiss Family Robinson" read either of those books again. They cannot go back to that time and remember how the scenes were unfolded, and again experience the emotions that they then did. The present reading will be dull and stale as compared with what they as boy and girl experienced. They may wonder how it was possible that they could have enjoyed such books. The shipwreck!, the island home!, the wonders of the island!—

those adventures were so real; but now—the colorful scenes have faded, the glamour has gone. And so fairy tales—they are entrancing. There were hours when the boy and girl read or heard read some marvelous account of what happened. The adventure of Jack and the Beanstalk, the victories of Jack, the Giant Killer, are alive to John, who may fancy himself as Jack, and do over again the wonders that Jack had done. Mary is delighted with the Sleeping Beauty in the enchanted palace, or with Cinderella. She herself may be the Beauty, awaiting the coming of the Prince; or, like Cinderella, watch the transformation of mice into horses and of a pumpkin into a coach and be carried to the palace—there to meet the Prince—if only a fairy godmother would appear and do these things for her.

Man and woman have forgotten, and they never can recall the fascination of these stories, the interest which they then had for them, as boy and girl.

The boy and girl also went through tragic experiences— and where is there man or woman who can understand or share the sorrows of a child! John had not returned from play. After a search he was found sitting on a rock, his head in his hands, his body shaking. And there at his feet lay the remains of his dog, Scraggy. Scraggy had once been struck by an auto and nearly killed. John had rescued the dog and nursed him back to life, and had named him Scraggy. Now, Scraggy had been struck again by a passing car—for the last time! Scraggy was dead, and John was disconsolate. Scraggy and he had understood each other; that was enough for John. No other dog could take his place with John. But in after years, when John had grown into the man and woman world, the tragedy is forgotten, the pathos gone; Scraggy is only a faint memory.

Mary comes running to her mother, sobbing as though her heart would break. And between her sobs she wails: "Oh Mother! Mother! Carlo has pulled off Peggy's leg. What shall I do? What shall I do?" She had shaken her rag doll at the dog while at play, and off came the leg when Carlo seized it. Mary bursts into a spasm of emotion and there is another flood of tears. The world is dark! The light has gone—with the loss of Peggy's leg. The mother tells Mary that she shall have a nicer and a prettier doll to take the place of Peggy. But this promise only adds to Mary's grief. "Nicer and prettier than Peggy? Indeed! Peggy is not ugly. There is no doll so nice, or as pretty, as Peggy." And Mary hugs closer the remainder of the rag doll. "Poor, dear Peggy!" Mary will not part with Peggy, now that she has lost her leg. The perplexed mother has forgotten her own rag doll that in the long ago she, too, had loved.

Man and woman seldom see in the child the future man or woman, as they watch the child in pensive mood, at pastime or at study. They cannot or do not try to enter the world in which the child lives, in which they at one time lived, and which they have outgrown and utterly forgotten. The man and woman world is a different world. The two worlds intersect, so that the inhabitants of both worlds may communicate with each other. Nevertheless, the inhabitants of these worlds merely sense each other; they do not understand. Why? Because a partition of forgetfulness separates the boy-and-girl-world from the man-and-woman-world.

The child leaves childhood when it passes through that partition and is then a man or a woman, but its age is not the determining factor. The partition may be passed at the adolescent period, or it may be before or after; it may not be until schooldays are over, or even after marriage—which depends on one's development, his morals, and on his mental capacities. But childhood is left behind by going through a blank, that partition. And a few human beings remain in the boy-and-girl-world all the days of their lives. With some it lasts no longer than a day or a month. But once the boy and girl stage is left behind and the man and woman stage has actually begun, the partition of forgetfulness closes behind them and shuts them off forever from the boy-and-girl-world. If ever man or woman is reminded of a vivid scene in that world, or of an event in which he or she had been much concerned, it is only a flash-like memory—which in a moment fades into the dim past of dreams.

Sooner or later, in every normal case, a critical change takes place. As long as the conscious something remains conscious that it is not the body in which it plays the part, it distinguishes itself from the body and the part. But as it continues to play, it gradually forgets the distinction and difference between itself and the part it plays. It no longer chooses to play parts. It thinks of itself as being the body; it identifies itself as the name of the body and with the part it plays. Then it ceases to be the actor, and is conscious of the body and the name and the part. At that time it may think itself out of the boy-and-girl-world and into the man-and-woman-world.

At times the conscious something becomes conscious that there is also a conscious something in each of the boys and girls with whom it is acquainted, and it may even be conscious of that in a man or in a woman. Then that conscious something is conscious that not one of these conscious somethings in the boy and girl or man and woman is conscious of itself *as* who and what it is, or whence it came. It learns that the conscious something in each boy or girl is in the same predicament in which it is; that is to say, they are conscious, but cannot explain to themselves who or what it is that is conscious, or how they are so conscious; that there are times when each must make-believe it is what it is not, and there are other times when necessity does not compel; and, that at these times it is allowed to make-believe what it pleases—then it revels in the world of make-believe, as fancy leads.

Then, with a few, there are moments—and with most these become less frequent or altogether cease with the passing of the year—when all is still, when time stops; it is not noticed; when no thing appears; sense-memory and the states of matter fade away; the world does not exist. Then the attention of the conscious something is fixed in itself; it is alone, and conscious.

20

There is the miracle: Oh! it *IS* itself, the timeless, the true, the eternal! Within that moment—it is gone. Breath continues, the heart beats, time goes on, clouds enclose, objects appear, sounds rush in, and the conscious something is again conscious of the body with a name and of its relations to other things, and it is again lost in the world of make-believe. Such a rare and in-between moment, like an unrelated reminiscence, comes unannounced. It may happen only once or many times in a life. It may happen just before sleep at night, or while it is becoming conscious of waking in the morning, or it may happen at any moment of the day and regardless of whatever activities there may be.

This conscious something may persist in being conscious of itself throughout the boy and girl period, and it may continue until it accepts the cares or the pleasures of life as its "realities." Indeed, in some few individuals it is indomitable and cannot surrender its feeling of identity to the engrossing senses of the body. It is the same conscious and distinct something through the entire life of the body. It does not know enough to make its identity known to itself so that it can distinguish itself from the body with a name. It may feel that this can be done, but it does not learn how to do it. Yet in these few individuals it will not or cannot cease to be conscious that it is not the body. The conscious something needs no argument or authority to convince it or assure it of this truth. That is too obvious to argue about. It is not bombastic or egotistic, but concerning this truth it is its own and only authority. The body in which it exists changes, objects change, its feelings and desires change; but, contrary to these and to all else, it is conscious that it is and always has been the very same identical conscious something as itself that has not changed and does not change, and that it is in no way affected by time.

There is a self-knowing Identity which is related to and is inseparable from the conscious something; but that Identity is not the conscious something, and it is not in the body, though it is in contact with the conscious something in the body which entered the body with a name, and which became conscious of the body it had entered, and conscious of the world. The conscious something comes into the body a few years after the birth of the body and leaves it at the death of that body. It is that which does things in the world, the Doer in the body. And after a time it will enter another body with a name, and still other bodies with other names, in the course of time. But the self-knowing Identity in contact with the conscious something in each of its existences, in each child, is the same self-knowing Identity by which the conscious something cannot help being conscious *of* itself, and, conscious during the early years of that body that it is *not* the body with a name. The conscious something in the body does not know *who* it is or *what* it is; it does not know the Identity or of its relation to the self-knowing Identity. It is conscious *as* the conscious something because of its relation to the Thinker-Knower of its Triune Self, its individual Trinity.

The self-knowing Identity is not born nor does it die when its conscious something enters a body or leaves the body; it is unchanged at each existence of its "conscious something," and it is undisturbed by death. In itself it is the calm, the serene, the everlasting Identity—of which presence the conscious something in the body is conscious. The conscious something is, then, the only self-evident fact or truth that one knows. But with most all persons the conscious something is invariably disguised and engulfed by the senses, and it is identified with the body and as the body.

For a man or woman to be again conscious *as* what he or she was conscious of when a little boy or girl, sense-memory is not enough. Merely to say they remember will not do. Memory, like a faint and indistinct dream, is of the past. The conscious something is essentially of the present, of the timeless Now. The desires and feelings of the man and of the woman are not conscious as they were in the boy and in the girl, and the thinking is different. Therefore, for the man and woman to understand why the boy and the girl do act as they do, the man would have to re-become and be conscious as the boy, and the woman would have to re-become and be conscious as the girl. This they cannot do. They cannot, because the conscious something which was then conscious that it was not the body or the part it played, makes no such distinction now. This lack of distinction is largely because the then undeveloped sexual organs of the boy might have influenced, but could not compel, the thinking of the conscious something in that boy. Now the same identical conscious something in the man is compelled to think in terms of the desires of a man, because his thinking and acting are suggested and colored and compelled by the organs and functions of a man. The same is true of a woman. The then undeveloped organs of the girl did influence, but they did not compel, the thinking of the conscious something. Now, the very same conscious something in the woman is compelled to think according to the feelings of a woman because her thinking and acting are colored and determined by the organs and functions of the woman. These facts, as cause, make it almost impossible for a man or woman to desire and feel and understand how the boy and the girl think, and why they act as they do in their world.

Boys and girls have fewer prejudices than men and women. You, as a boy or as a girl, had few or no prejudices at all. The reason is that you had not at that time formed definite beliefs of your own, and you had not had time to accept as your own beliefs the beliefs of your parents or of the people you met. Naturally, you had likes and dislikes and these you changed from time to time as you listened to the likes and dislikes shown by your companions and by older people, but more especially by your father and mother. You very much wished to have things explained, because you wanted to understand. You were ready to change any belief if you could get anyone to give you a reason or to assure you that what they said was true. But you probably learned, as children usually learn, that the ones you asked to explain did not want to bother to explain, or that they thought you would not understand, or that they were unable to tell you what you wanted to know. You were free from prejudice then. Today you are most likely carrying a large stock of prejudices, although you may be horrified to admit the fact until you begin to think about it. If you do think about it you will find that you have family, racial, national, political, social and other prejudices concerning everything that has to do with human activities. These you have acquired since the time you were a boy or a girl. Prejudices are among the most distinguished and cherished of human characteristics.

There is a constant intermingling of boys and girls with men and women. Yet, all sense a difference, an invisible barrier of the world-of-men-and-women from the world-of-boys-and-girls. And that barrier remains until there is a change in the boy and in the girl. The change from boy and girl to man and woman is sometimes gradual, very gradual. And sometimes the change is sudden. But the change is sure to come in every human being who does not remain a child throughout life. The boy and the girl are conscious of the change when it comes, though some do forget it later on. Before the change, the boy may have said: I want to be a man, and the girl: I wish I were a woman. After the change, the boy declares: I am a man, and the girl: I am now a woman. And the parents and others will see and perhaps comment on the change. What has caused or brought about this change, this critical state, this crossing of the barrier, which is the partition-of-forgetfulness, separating the boy-and-girl-world from the man-and-woman-world? How is the partition made or prepared, and how is it put into place?

Thinking designs the partition, thinking prepares it, and thinking establishes its place. The change from boy and girl into man and woman must be twofold: the change in the

24

physical development of their sexes, and the concomitant change in their mental development, by thinking. Physical growth and sexual development will take the boy and girl to the man-and-woman-world, and there they will be man and woman in so far as their sexes are concerned. But unless they have by their own thinking made a corresponding advance in mental development, they will not cross the bar. They will still be in the boy-and-girl-world. Physical sexual development without mental development disqualifies them as man and woman. Thus they remain: man and woman sexually, but boy and girl mentally, in the boy-and-girl-world. They appear to be man and woman. But they are irresponsible. They are unfortunate facts to both worlds. They have outgrown and developed beyond the child state and are no longer children. But they lack mental responsibility, have no sense or understanding of right and fitness, and cannot therefore be depended upon as man and as woman.

To cross the partition-of-forgetfulness from boy and girl, and to enter into the man-and-woman-world, thinking must accompany and correspond to the sexual development. The partition is made and adjusted by two processes of thinking. The conscious something in the body does the thinking. One of the two processes is carried on by the conscious something in progressively identifying or relating itself to the sexual development or sexual function of the man body or the woman body in which it is. This identification is confirmed by the conscious something as it continues to think of itself as that body and as that function. The other process of thinking is the acceptance by the conscious something of what are sometimes called the cold and hard facts of life, and by the identifying of itself as the bodily personality on which it depends for food and possessions and a name and place in the world, and for the power to be, to will, to do, and to have all these; or, to be and to have such of these as it wills.

When, by thinking, the conscious something in the boy or in the girl has identified itself with the sexual body in which it is, and makes itself dependent for a name and place and power in the world, then come the critical state, moment and event. This is a third thinking, and it comes in lowly and in high estate. It is when the conscious something decides what is his or her position in the world, and what that position is in relation to other men and women. This third and determining thinking is the factor or self-contract of the conscious something with the body it is in, and with the relation of that body to other human bodies and to the world. This thinking causes and creates a certain mental attitude of moral responsibility. This third thinking coalesces the sexual and bodily identity with the conditions of living. This thinking or attitude of mind precipitates, lays and fixes. Then the boy or girl which was, is out of the boy-and-girl-world, and is now a man or a woman in the man-and-woman-world.

The boy-and-girl-world vanishes as they become more and more conscious of themselves and their activities as man and woman. The world is the same old world; it has not changed. But because they have changed from boy and girl into man and woman, and because they see the world through their eyes as man and as woman, the world seems to be different. They see things now which they could not see when they were boy and girl. And all the things of which they were then conscious, they are now conscious of in a different way. The young man and woman do not make comparisons or question themselves about the differences. They are conscious of things as things appear to them to be, and which they accept as facts, and each one deals with the facts according to his or her individual make-up. Life seems to be opening up to them, according to their natures and to the social stratum in which they are, and it seems to continue to open as they go on.

Now what happened to the young man and woman to make them see the world and the things in it to be so different?

Well, on going through the partition-of-forgetfulness they at once became conscious of a line of demarcation, which divided the man side from the woman side of the man-and-woman-world. The young man and the young woman did not say: I will take this side, or, I will take that side, of the line. They said nothing about the matter. The young man saw himself to be and was conscious of himself as being a man on the man side, and the young woman saw herself to be and was conscious of herself as being a woman on the woman side of the line dividing man from woman. This is the way of life and growth. It is as though life were a section on a circular-time-moving-roadway onto which baby boys and baby girls are ushered. They laugh and cry and grow and play, while the roadway moves them on through the period of the boy-and-girl-world up to the line of demarcation which runs through the entire boy-and-girl- and the man-and-woman-worlds. But the boy and girl do not see the line until they go through the partition-of-forgetfulness. The boy keeps on the road, but on the man side of the line. The girl also keeps on the road, and on the woman side of the dividing line. So on each side of the line they go as man and as woman into the man-and-woman-world. Men and women look at each other and they intermingle on the visible section of the circular-time-moving-roadway called life until the very end, the man being always conscious of his side and the woman of her side. Then death is the end of the visible physical-life-section of the roadway. The visible physical body is left on the visible section of the road. But the circular-time-moving-roadway carries on the conscious something with its invisible form through many after-death states and periods and leaves all invisible bodies and forms on their particular sections of the road. The circular-time-moving-roadway continues. Again it brings on to its visible section called life, another baby boy or baby girl. And, in its turn, again that same conscious something enters that boy or girl to carry on with its purpose through the visible section of the roadway.

Of course, boys and girls are conscious, more or less, that there is a difference between a boy and a girl; but they do not bother their heads overly much about the difference. But when their bodies become men and women their heads bother them about the difference. Men and women cannot forget the difference. Their bodies will not let them forget.

The world is fast or the world is slow. But whether fast or slow—that is the way that man and woman make it go. Over and over again beyond the record of time a civilization has risen; and always it has fallen and faded away. What is the purpose! What is the gain! Must the rise and fall of civilization after civilization continue through the endless future! Its religions, ethics, politics, laws, literature, arts, and sciences; its manufacture, commerce and other essentials to civilization, have been based upon and depend upon man and woman.

And now another civilization—supposed to be the greatest of all civilizations—is rising, and is being raised to greater and ever greater heights—by man and woman. And must it, too, fall? Its fate depends on man and woman. It need not fail and fall. If it is changed from its impermanence and is built for permanence, it will not fail; it cannot fall!

The United States of America is to be the battleground of this civilization, on which the future of the nations will be worked out. But man and woman can build a civilization only according to what they know about themselves. Man and woman know that they were born and that they will die. This is one of the causes of the failure and the fall of past civilizations. That in them which makes them man and woman does not die. It lives beyond the grave. It comes again, and again it goes. And as often as it goes, it returns.

To build for permanence, man and woman must understand and discern and become familiar with the immortal something in them which does not, cannot, die when its appearances as man and woman have run their course and there

28

is an end of days. That conscious thing, that deathless something, periodically dreams itself into an appearance as a man or as a woman. In its dream it seeks the reality which it lost—the other side of itself. And not finding it in its own appearance, it seeks it in the other appearance—the man body or the woman body. Alone, and without that lost reality of which it dreams, it feels incomplete. And it hopes to find and to have happiness and completion in the appearance of the man or of the woman.

Seldom or never do a man and a woman live happily together. But seldom, if ever, do man and woman live happily apart. What a paradox: Man and woman are not happy with each other, and they are unhappy without each other. With the experience of countless lives of dreaming, man and woman have not worked out the solution to their two problems: How to be happy with each other; and, how to be happy without each other.

Because of the unhappiness and restlessness of man and woman with or without each other, the people of every land continue to be in hope and fear, doubt and insecurity, with only an appearance of joyousness, resourcefulness, and confidence. In public and in private, there is plotting and planning; there is running here and running there, to get and to get and never to be satisfied. Greed is hidden by a mask of generosity; vice smirks beside public virtue; deceit, hatred, dishonesty, fear, and falsehood are clothed in fair words to lure and trap the wary and astute; and organized crime brazenly stalks and gets its prey in public light of day while law lags behind.

Man and woman build for food, or for possessions, or for a name, or for power, to satisfy man and woman. They never can be satisfied, as merely man and woman. Prejudice, jealousy, guile, envy, lust, anger, hatred, malice, and the seeds of these are now being laid and built into the structure of this rising civilization. If not removed or changed, the thoughts of these will inevitably flower and exteriorize as war and disease,

and death will be the end of man and woman and their civilization; and the earth and the water about all lands will leave
little or no trace of its having existed. If this civilization is to go
on and to bridge that break in the rise and fall of civilizations,
man and woman must discern the permanence in their bodies
and in nature; they must learn what that deathless something
in them is; they must understand that it has no sex; they must
understand why it makes man man and woman woman; and
why and how the dreamer is now in appearance a man or a
woman.

Nature is vast—mysterious beyond the dreams of man or
woman. And the more that is known, the more is shown the
little that is known, as compared to what there is to be known
of the vastnesses and mysteries of nature. Praise without stint
is due to the men and women who have added to the fund in
that treasury of knowledge called science. But the intricacies
and complexities of nature will increase with the continuance
of discovery and invention. Distance, measure, weight, size,
are not to be trusted as rules for the understanding of nature.
There is a purpose throughout nature, and all operations of
nature are for the carrying on of that purpose. Man and woman
know something about some of the changes in nature, but they
do not know about the continuity of purpose and permanence
through nature, because they do not know the continuity and
permanence of themselves.

Human memory is of the four senses: seeing, hearing,
tasting, and smelling. Memory of the Self is of The Eternal:
continuity uninterrupted by the changes of time, beginning-
lessness and endlessness; that is, The Eternal Order of Progression.

Man and woman lost the knowledge they formerly had
about themselves and about the permanence in nature, and
ever since, they have been wanderers in ignorance and trouble
throughout the labyrinths and changes of this man-and-
woman-world. Man and woman can continue their wander-

ings if they choose, but they also can, and sometime they will, begin to find their way out of the labyrinth of deaths and births and become acquainted with the knowledge that is to be theirs—and which awaits them. The man or woman who would come into possession of that knowledge can carefully consider the outline of nature and the origin and history of themselves, and about how they lost their way and came to be in the man and woman bodies they are in today.

It will be well here to consider briefly man's place in the all-embracing scheme of things, beings and Intelligences, within the One Reality: *Consciousness Absolute*; that is, the Doer's relation, on the one hand, to nature and, on the other hand, to the immortal Triune Self, of which he is a part. However, as both nature and the human being are extraordinarily complex, it is not feasible or necessary for present purposes to more than briefly sketch their many divisions and parts.

There are four basic, primordial "elements" out of which all things and beings have come. For lack of more specific terms, they are here spoken of as the elements of fire, air, water, and earth. These terms do not connote what is commonly understood by them.

The elements are made up of countless units. A unit is an indivisible, indestructible, irreducible ONE. Units are either unintelligent on the nature-side, or intelligent on the intelligent-side of the great cosmos.

Nature, on the nature-side, is a machine composed of the totality of nature units, which are conscious *as* their function only.

There are four kinds of nature units: free units, transient units, compositor units, and sense units. Free units may pass anywhere in nature, in streams of flowing units, but they are not detained by the things through which they pass. Transient units combine with other units and are held for a time; they are made to enter, and thus build into visibility and tangibility, the inner structure and the outer appearance of mineral, plant, animal and human bodies, where they remain for a while, to be replaced by others; and then they flow on again in streams of transient units. Some of the manifestations of transient units are the nature forces, such as gravity, electricity, magnetism, and lightning. Compositor units compose transient units according to abstract forms; they build the bodies of cells, organs and the four systems in the human body—the generative, respiratory, circulatory and digestive systems. The fourth kind of nature units, sense units, are the senses of sight, hearing, taste and smell, which control the four systems and relate the objects of nature to them.

In addition to these four kinds of nature units there is, in the human and there only, the breath-form unit—a descriptive term for what is spoken of as the "living soul." The form part of the breath-form is usually referred to when the "soul" and, in psychology, the "subconscious" or "unconscious" are being considered; the breath part of the breath-form is the breath which enters the infant's body with the first gasp. No animal has a breath-form.

There is only one breath-form unit in each human body. It remains with that body during life, and at death it accompanies the Doer of the Triune Self into the early after-death states; later it joins the Doer again as that Doer makes ready for another life on earth. The breath-form unit coordinates the four senses with the four systems and keeps in working relation all the units of the body. The breath-form occupies the front or anterior half of the pituitary body in the brain. From there it controls and coordinates all the involuntary functions of the body, and in the rear half it is in direct contact with the conscious something in the body—the Doer of the Triune Self.

And then there is a unit which relates the intelligent-side to the nature-side in the human being, called the aia. During life the aia serves as intermediary between the breath-form and the Doer in the body; in the after-death states it performs certain definite functions and, when the time comes for the Doer to re-exist, the aia enables the breath-form to cause conception and, later, birth of the body.

The human being as a whole is on the intelligent-side of the universe, by virtue of being inhabited by the Doer part of an immortal being, an individual trinity, here called the Triune Self. In every man or woman there is the self-exiled part of a self-knowing and immortal Triune Self. This Triune Self, this individual—not universal—trinity has, as the name implies, three parts: the Knower or identity and knowledge, the noetic part; the Thinker or rightness and reason, the mental part; and the Doer or feeling and desire, the psychic part. In every man and woman there is a portion of the Doer part of a Triune Self. The Doer re-exists in one human body after another, and thus lives from life to life, separated by periods in many states after death. This alternating between life on earth and life in after-death states is exemplified by states of waking and sleeping. All are states of the Doer who is present and conscious. A point of difference is that after death the Doer does not return to the body now dead, but must wait until a new body has been prepared by the future parents and is made ready to receive the Doer.

There is that within the dim and forgotten history of every human being which caused the Doer in every man and woman to become the self-exiled part of its self-knowing and immortal Triune Self. Long, long ago, Knower, Thinker and Doer were one inseparable, immortal Triune Self, in The Realm of Permanence, commonly spoken of as Paradise, or The Garden of Eden, in a sexless, perfect "Adam"-body of balanced units, in the interior of the earth—which body, being perfect, is often referred to as the "first temple, not made with human hands."

Briefly, this self-exile from The Realm of Permanence came about by the failure of all those Doers who subsequently became human beings, to pass a certain test, which it was necessary for all Doers to pass, in order to complete the individual Triune Selves. This failure constituted the so-called "original sin," in that "Adam," or rather Adam and Eve in their twin bodies, suffered the "fall of man." By their failure to pass that test, they were expelled from "Paradise" in the interior of the earth onto the outer crust of the earth.

The multitudes of Doers who thus "sinned" live as men and women in their human bodies, subject to the need of material food, and to birth and death, and death and birth. The balanced units of their previously sexless bodies had become unbalanced, and were what they are now, male-female and female-male, and the Doers were men and women—or desire-feeling and feeling-desire, as will be explained further on.

To continue briefly with man's relation to the Universe and to nature: the Universe, with its four pre-chemical elements—fire, air, water and earth—is composed of nature units and intelligent units. The four kinds of nature units—free, transient, compositor, and sense units—are the structure-stuff of all things, objects and bodies in the great nature machine. All nature units are in ceaseless motion, and all take part in a slow, very slow, but progressive development, the number being constant and unchangeable. Nature units are conscious *as* their functions only, but the units on the intelligent-side are conscious *of* or *as* what they are.

There are limits to the progress of nature units, the most advanced nature units being the senses of sight, hearing, taste and smell. The next degree is that of the breath-form unit, which accompanies the Doer through life and death and, in life, is the direct medium of communication between the Doer and nature. It has an active and a passive side, the active side being the breath, and the passive side being the abstract form of the body. With the first cry at birth until the last gasp at death, the breath, which is fourfold, surrounds and flows in and out and through every part of the physical body.

34

Perfection—the secret and unknown goal of human striving—means that the now unbalanced units of the human body will have been balanced; that is, they will no longer be male or female, but will be made up of sexless, balanced, cells. Then the Doer will again be in its perfect body; it will not be subject to disease and death and will not need gross material food, but will be sustained and nourished by breathing of the life eternal, uninterrupted by periods of sleep or death. The Doer will then be in accord with his Thinker-Knower, in a perfect body of eternal youth—the second temple—in The Realm of Permanence, The Eternal.

By reviewing its forgotten history, the immortal Doer in the body of every man and woman may understand how it exiled itself from its Triune Self in The Realm of Permanence and is now lost in the body—a wanderer in the man-and-woman-world of birth and death and rebirth.

To show how all this came about, and that it is possible for the human being to take up again the thread that was broken in the dim past, and thereby to take the first steps for a return to The Realm of Permanence, is a purpose of this book.

PART II

THE CHILD: "Mother, Where Did I Come From?" and: How to Help the Child Remember

The making of machines and the tools to make machines marks the beginning of civilization. The pivot, lever, sled, and wheel of primitive times, no less than the intricately complicated and delicately adjusted instruments and mechanisms which have helped to make civilization what it is, have been brought into existence by the thinking and the thoughts of man.

Man's accomplishments with machines have been so great, and he has been so successful in the invention of new machines, that he sometimes assumes that nearly all things are machines. The machine so dominates man's thinking that the period has been designated the machine age.

A modern psychologist was asked: "Do you mean to say that you consider man to be a machine—and nothing more than a machine?"

And he answered: "Yes, we mean just that."

"Then a term more suited to your study would be mechanology. Your term psychology is a misnomer. You cannot have a psychology without a psyche."

When asked for a definition of psychology, he answered: "Psychology is the study of human behavior. 'Soul!' No, we do not use the word soul. If soul is not the body, we do not know anything about the soul. For over two thousand years philosophers have talked about a soul, and in all that time they have not proved that there is such a thing as 'soul'; they have not even told us just what a soul is. We modern psychologists could not study an alleged thing about which we know nothing. We decided to stop talking about what we do not know, and to study something about which we do know, that is, man as a physical organism which receives impressions through the senses and which responds to the impressions received."

It is true! People have talked about a soul without being able to say what a soul is or what it does. No definite meaning has been given to the word "soul." Soul is not descriptive of any act or quality or thing. The word "Doer" is here used when "soul" would ordinarily be employed to indicate a connection with "God." But the term "breath-form" has been coined—instead of soul—as descriptive of certain very definite functions, prenatally, during life and in the early after-death states.

Man has made a robot as evidence that man is a machine, and that a machine could be made that would do the things that man does. But a robot is not a human machine, nor is a human machine a robot. The human machine is a living machine and it does respond to impressions received through its senses, but it responds because there is a conscious something inside, which feels and wills and operates the machine. That conscious something is the Doer. When the Doer in the body is cut off from the machine or quits it, the machine cannot respond because it is an inanimate body and cannot be made to do anything of itself.

A robot is a machine, but it is not a living machine; it has no senses, is not conscious, and there is no conscious something inside to operate it. What a robot does, it is made to do by the thinking and the acting of the Doer in a living human body.

Man would like to breathe the breath of life into his robot, even as Pygmalion tried to give life to his ivory statue, Galatea. But he cannot do that, and he cannot pray—as Pygmalion did to Aphrodite to give life to the object of his own fashioning—because, believing that he is a machine only, there is nothing to which a machine could pray.

However, the body of every man and woman actually is a machine, made up of many parts which are coordinated into one living, self-functioning whole. Briefly, these parts take in four systems—the generative, respiratory, circulatory, and digestive systems—and the systems are made up of organs, the organs of cells, the cells of molecules, the molecules of atoms, and the atoms of still smaller particles, such as electrons, protons and positrons. And each of these infinitesimally small particles is a unit, an irreducible and indivisible One.

But what is it that composes all those constituents into, and controls, the living man and woman body? That is indeed one of the great mysteries of human life.

The unit doing this is the "breath-form." The term includes and expresses succinctly its functions and the idea which other terms currently in vogue are intended to convey, such as the "subconscious mind" and the "soul." The breath-form is the coordinator and general manager of the human body, and the human being is the only creature possessed of a breath-form; no animal has a breath-form, but the model or type of every breath-form is many times modified and extended into the animal and vegetable kingdoms of nature. All kingdoms of nature are dependent on the types of man and woman; thus all forms of life are, in an ever-descending scale, modifications and variations of the man and woman types.

For a conception to take place during the union of man and woman, a breath-form must be present. Then, through their breaths, the form of the breath-form enters into and relates, and then or later bonds, the spermatozoon of the man body and the ovum of the woman body. The bonding of the man and woman cells by the breath-form is the beginning of what will eventually become a man body or a woman body.

The sperm of the man body is the entire man body and its hereditary tendencies, reduced to the minutest model of the man body. The ovum of the woman is the smallest model of the woman body, bearing the impressions of all its antecedents.

As soon as the breath-form bonds the spermatozoon and the ovum, its potential two sides become actual, as an active side and a passive side. The active side is the breath; the passive side is the form of the body to be built.

Each breath-form belongs or is related to an individual conscious self, whose pending re-existence calls forth the breath-form from a temporary state of inertia to serve the same Doer once again during a term of life on earth.

The active side of the breath-form, as breath, starts the spark of life which unites the two cells of the future parents; and the passive side, as form, is the form or pattern or design according to which the united two cells begin to build. They build to order a special machine for the Doer who will live in, and keep alive, and manage that body. However, the breath of the breath-form does not enter the fetus itself during gestation, but throughout this period it is present with the mother in her atmosphere or aura, and through her breath causes the building and impressing on the form what the Doer who is to live in the new body has made its physical destiny. But, at the birth of the body, the breath of the breath-form enters the body itself with the first gasp as the breath of that body, and at the same time an extraordinary phenomenon takes place, in that an opening in the partition dividing the right and the left auricle (antechamber) of the heart closes, thereby changing the circulation in the infant's body and establishing it as the individual breath of that body.

During life, the breath and the form of the breath-form or "living soul" carry on the life and the growth of the body, which is to be followed by its decline and death when the breath-form unit leaves the body. Then again, the breath-form enters a state of inertia which intervenes between the life just ended and the next following life on earth of that Doer.

Upon entering the body, the breath penetrates and surrounds the body and pervades the inconceivable multitudes of units of matter of which the body is composed.

Actually, the breath is fourfold, but for the purposes of this book it is not necessary to mention here more than the physical breath, which is the only breath ordinarily used by the human being. It is not essential to know all the mechanics of the breath in order to work wonders in the body and in the world with the breath. But it is necessary to understand about feeling-and-desire, the Doer in the body, the psychic part of the Triune Self, in order to do more with the body than is ordinarily done.

Feeling in the body is that which *feels* and is conscious *of* itself but not *as* itself, and is the medium by which the work of one's life is carried on. Feeling is directly connected by means of the breath-form with the body through the voluntary nervous system, and with exterior nature through the involuntary nervous system. Thus are received impressions from nature and responses made from feeling in the body.

Desire in the body is the active side of feeling, and feeling is the passive side of desire in the body. *Desire is conscious power*, the only power by which changes are brought about in itself and in all other things. What is said of feeling in relation to the breath-form can also be said of desire. Feeling cannot act without desire, and desire cannot act without feeling. Feeling is in the nerves and the nervous system, and desire is in the blood and the circulatory system.

41

Feeling and desire are inseparable, but in both man and woman one predominates over the other. In the man, desire predominates over feeling; in the woman, feeling predominates over desire.

Why is it that man and woman can seldom or never agree when they are together for any length of time, and that they can seldom, if ever, live apart and be contented for a long time? One reason is that the man body and the woman body are so constituted and constructed that each body is incomplete in itself and is dependent on the other by sexual attraction. Sex attraction has its immediate cause in the cells and in the organs and in the senses of the man body and the woman body, and its remote cause is in the Doer in the body who operates the body. Another reason is that the desire side in the man body is attuned to the masculine body and suppresses or dominates its feeling side, and that the feeling side of the Doer in the woman body is attuned to the feminine body and suppresses or dominates its desire side. Then the desire in the man body, unable to get satisfaction from its feeling side, seeks union with a woman body expressing feeling. Likewise, the feeling of the Doer expressed in the woman body, unable to get satisfaction from its suppressed desire side, seeks satisfaction by union with the man body expressing desire.

The sexual cells and organs and senses force the desire of the Doer in the man body to desire the woman body, and the sexual cells and organs and senses force the feeling in the woman to want a man body. The man and the woman are irresistibly compelled by their bodies to think of each other. The desire in the man does not distinguish itself from the body it operates, and the feeling in the woman does not distinguish itself from the body it operates. Each of the bodies is electrically and magnetically so constructed and related that it attracts the other body, and this attraction compels the Doer in the body to think of the other and to seek satisfaction from the body of the other. The organs and the cells and the senses of each body drive or pull it to the other body by sex attraction.

When the Doer and the breath-form quit the body, they pass together into the early after-death states; the body is then dead. It disintegrates slowly and its constituents return to the elements of nature. After the Doer has gone through the Judgment, the breath-form enters a temporary state of inertia, until the time comes for the Doer to re-exist once more on earth.

When the Doer and the breath-form quit the body, the body is dead; it is a corpse. The Doer in the body operates the body but does not control it. Actually, the body controls the Doer because the Doer, not distinguishing itself from the body, is driven by the cells and the organs and the senses of the body to do what they demand and urge. The senses of the body suggest the objects of nature and urge feeling and desire to crave the objects. Then the Doer operates the body-mind to direct the bodily functions to get the objects or results desired.

At times the Doer in both a man and a woman body is conscious that there is a difference between itself and its body; it invariably knows that it is not the bodily senses which excite, cloud and befuddle it. It is not the name of its body. Then the man or woman stops to wonder, to ponder, and to think: Who or what is this elusive, mysterious but ever present "I" that is present in thinking and feeling and speaking, that seems to be so different at different times, and who now contemplates itself! "I" was a child! "I" went to school. In the flush of youth "I" did that! And that! And that! "I" had a father and a mother! Now "I" have children! "I" do this! And that! In the future it is possible that "I" will be so different from what "I" am now, that "I" cannot say with certainty what "I" then will be! "I" have been so many different things or beings other than that which "I" now am, that it stands to reason that "I" in the future will be as different from what "I" am now, as "I" am now different from each of the many beings which "I" was in the past. Certainly "I" should expect to change with time and condition and place! But the indisputable fact is, that with all, and through all, the changes, "I" have been and "I" am now, the self-same identical "I"!—unchanged, through all the changes!

Almost, the Doer had awaked to its reality *as* itself. It had almost distinguished and identified itself. But again, the senses shut it in and cloud it into sleep. And it continues its dream of itself as the body, and of the interests of the body.

The Doer who is harnessed up with the senses of the body will drive and drive—to do, to get, to have, or to be—from apparent necessity or for the sake of accomplishment. And so the busy dream of itself continues, with perhaps an occasional almost-waking of the Doer, life after life and civilization after civilization; ignorance of itself prevails from the dawn of civilization, and it increases with the pace of a civilization based on the senses. The ignorance in which parents have been bred is the ignorance in which they rear their children. Ignorance is the first cause of dissension and strife, and of the troubles of the world.

The Doer's ignorance of itself can be dispelled by the true Light—the Light which is itself not seen but which shows things as they are. The Light can be found by educating the young child, and through the child the true Light will come into the world and will eventually enlighten the world. The education of the child is not to begin in the schools of learning; its education must begin at its mother's side or with the guardian in whose charge it is.

The conscious something is conscious of innumerable acts, objects, and events; but of all the things of which it is conscious, there is one fact, and one fact only, that it knows beyond doubt or question. That mysterious and simple fact is: I am conscious! No amount of argument or thinking can disprove that one incontrovertible and self-evident fact as a truth. All other things may be questioned and discredited. But the conscious something in the body *knows* itself to be conscious. Beginning at its point of knowledge, that it is conscious, the conscious something can take one step on the path of real knowledge, self-knowledge. And it does take that step, by thinking. By thinking of its knowledge of being conscious, the conscious something at once becomes conscious that it is conscious.

A nature unit cannot progress beyond the degrees in being conscious *as* its functions. If a nature unit could be conscious *of* anything, no dependence could be put on a "law" of nature.

To be conscious, and be conscious that one is conscious, is as far as any human being can travel on the path of self-knowledge. It is possible for the conscious something in the human to take a second step on the path of its self-knowledge, but it is not probable that it will.

The second step on the path of its self-knowledge can be taken by asking and by answering the question: What is it that is conscious, and knows that it is conscious? The question is asked by thinking, and it can be answered by thinking of the question only—and of nothing but the question. To answer the question, the conscious something must isolate itself from the body; that is, be dis-attached from the body; and it is possible for it to do that by thinking. Then it will find itself as the feeling side of the Doer and it will know *what* it is, because the body and the senses will have been switched off, disconnected, and put aside for the time being. Nature cannot then hide the conscious something from itself, nor confuse it, nor make it believe that it is the body or the senses of the body. Then the conscious something can and will again take on the body and will use the senses, but it will no longer make the mistake of supposing itself to be the body and the senses. Then it can find and can take all the other steps on the path of self-knowledge. The way is straight and simple, but it is beset by impassable obstacles to one who has not indomitable will. Yet, there is no limit to the knowledge one may have if he will learn and use his power to think.

The way man and woman have been brought up is a reason why it is almost, if not quite, impossible, for the conscious something in the body to find itself by isolating itself from the body, and so to know *what* it is. The reason is that the conscious something cannot think without using the body-mind in its thinking, because the body-mind will not let it.

Here a few words are needed about the "mind." The human being has not only one mind, but three minds, that is, three ways of thinking: the body-mind, to think with for the body and the objects of the senses only; the feeling-mind, for the feeling of the Doer; and the desire-mind, to think for and about the desire of the Doer.

Every time the conscious something tries to think of itself with its feeling-mind or desire-mind, the body-mind projects into its thinking impressions of objects of the senses of which it had been conscious during the life of that body.

The body-mind cannot tell the conscious something anything about itself and its Triune Self. The conscious something cannot suppress the functions of the body-mind, because the body-mind is stronger than its desire-mind or its feeling-mind. The body-mind is stronger and has advantage and ascendancy over the other two minds because it was developed and given precedence during childhood, when the parents told the conscious something that it was the body. Since then, the body-mind has been in constant and habitual use, and it dominates all thinking.

There is a way to make it possible, and even probable, for the conscious something to become conscious *as* itself, as different and distinct from the body. To stop the body-mind from controlling the conscious something and so hindering its knowledge of itself, it must be helped by its parents in early childhood. This help should begin when the conscious some-

46

thing comes into the child and asks the mother such questions as, who and what it is and where it came from. If the conscious something does not receive the proper answers it will not continue the questions, and will later be hypnotized by the parents, and it will hypnotize itself into believing that it is the body with a name. Its education in self-knowledge should begin as soon as it begins to ask about itself, and it should be helped until it can carry on its own education in self-knowledge.

Parents, in their childhood, were instructed in the tenets of their religions. They were told that an almighty God who created heaven and earth also created a special "soul" for each human which He puts into every baby that is born to man and woman. Just what that soul is has not been explained so that one can understand. It is affirmed that the soul is a finer part of the physical, or another finer body, because it is taught that that finer body continues its existence after the death of the fleshly body. The parent has also been instructed that after death the soul will enjoy reward or suffer punishment for what it did on earth. The parents who believe, simply believe. They do not understand the commonplace occurrences of birth and death. Therefore, after a while they no longer try to understand. They can only believe. They are admonished not to try to understand the mystery of life and death; that that mystery is in the keeping of Almighty God alone and not to be known by mankind. Therefore, when the child has reached the stage where it asks its mother who it is and what it is and where it came from, the mother in days gone by has given it the old, old untruths as answers. But in this modern day and generation, some children will not be evaded; they persist in questioning. So the modern mother tells her modern child such new untruths as she thinks her child will understand. Here is a conversation which took place in modern fashion:

"Mother," said little Mary, "every time I ask you where I came from or how you got me, you put me off, or tell me some story, or tell me to stop asking such questions. Now, Mother, you must know! You do know! And I want you to tell me who I am. Where did I come from, and how did you get me?"

And the Mother answered: "Very well, Mary. If you must know, I will tell you. And I hope it will satisfy you. When you were a very little girl I bought you in a department store. Since then you have been growing up; and, if you are not a nice little girl and do not learn to behave yourself, I will take you back to that store and exchange you for another little girl."

One smiles at the story of how Mary's mother got Mary. But Mary was stunned, and sorrowful, as are most children who are told similar stories. Such moments ought not to be forgotten. That mother lost a great opportunity to help the conscious something in her child to be conscious *as* itself. Millions of mothers make no use of such opportunities. Instead, they are untruthful to their children. And from their parents, the children learn to be untruthful; they learn to distrust their parents.

A mother does not wish to be untruthful. She does not wish to teach her child to be untruthful. What she says is usually what she remembers her own mother or other mothers to have said, who smile as they confide to each other how they elude or baffle their children when they ask questions about their origin.

Never a moment passes when there is not somewhere in this world an eager, anxious, and sometimes a disconsolate, lonesome conscious something, away from the other parts of itself and in solitude, asking as in a dream through the child body in which it finds itself: Who am I? Where did I come from? How did I get here?—asking in this dream world in the forlorn hope of eliciting an answer that will help it to awaken to the reality of itself. Its hopes are invariably blasted by the replies to its questions. Then kind forgetfulness and time as constantly heal the wounds received in such tragic moments. And the conscious something accustoms itself to dream on while it lives, and it is not conscious that it dreams.

The education of the men and women of the future should begin with the child when it asks such questions. Falsehood and deceit are practiced on the conscious something by the guardians of its body in which it finds residence as soon as it begins to ask questions about itself.

From necessity the child is obliged to adapt itself to its changing body, to the customs of living, and to the habits and opinions of others. Gradually it is made to believe that it is the body in which it exists. From the time it was conscious of its existence in the world until the time it identifies itself as the man or woman body, and with the name of that body, the conscious something as that man or as that woman has been going through a training and has been accustoming itself to the belief and the practice of falsehood and deceit, and thus hypocrisy is acquired. Falsehood, deceit and hypocrisy are everywhere condemned and denounced, yet for place and position in the world they are secret arts to be privately practiced by the knowing ones.

The man or woman of the world who has retained some of the pristine honesty and truthfulness of the conscious something in the body, through all the shocks and checks and falsehoods and deceits practiced upon it by enemies and friends, is a man or woman most rare. It is seen that it is almost impossible to live in the world and not to practice hypocrisy, deceit and falsehood. Depending on the destiny and the cycle, that one may stand out a living monument in the history of man or pass on unnoticed and obscure.

What is styled education is the opposite of education. Education is or should be a method to educe—to draw out, improve and develop—from the child the character, faculties, qualities, aptitudes and other potentialities that are latent in the child. What is spoken of as education is a prescribed set of instructions, rules and ruts which the child is schooled to memorize and to practice. Instead of drawing out what is in the child, the instruction has a tendency to bottle up and stifle in the child its inherent and potential knowledge, to make it imitative and artificial instead of spontaneous and original. To make self-knowledge available to the man, instead of restricting him to the schooling of sense-knowledge, his education should begin when still a child.

A clear distinction should be made between the baby and the child. The baby period begins at birth and lasts until it asks and answers questions. The child period begins when it asks questions about itself, and it continues until the end of adolescence. The baby is trained; the child should be educated, and training precedes education.

The baby's training consists of guiding it in the use of its four senses: to see, to hear, to taste, to smell; to remember what it sees, hears, tastes and smells; and to articulate and repeat the words it hears. Feeling is not a fifth sense; it is one of the two aspects of the Doer.

Not all mothers are aware that at first their babies do not see or hear correctly. But after a while, if the mother will dangle or move an object before the baby, she can notice that if the eyes are glassy or if they do not follow the object the baby does not see; that if the eyes bob or wobble, the baby senses the object but is unable to focus on or see the object; that the baby cannot sense distances if it reaches out and clutches at a distant object. When the mother speaks to the infant, she learns from the glazed eye and blank face that it does not see, or she learns by the smiling face and baby eyes looking into hers that it sees. So it is also with tastes and smells. The tastes are unpleasant or pleasant and the smells are merely disagreeable or comforting, until the baby is trained into its likes and dislikes. The mother points, and carefully says, "Cat! Dog! Boy!" And the baby is to repeat these or other words or sentences.

There is a time when the baby is not looking out or pointing at things, or repeating words, or playing with rattles. It may be silent, or seeming to be wondering, or appear to be in reverie. This is the end of the baby period and the beginning of the period of childhood. The change is caused by the nearness of, or coming of, the conscious something into the body. The child may be silent or it may act strangely for a day or many days. During this time the conscious something senses that some strange thing surrounds it and clouds and confuses it, as in a dream, where it cannot remember where it is. It feels lost. After it fails in its struggles with itself to find itself, it asks, probably its mother: Who am I? What am I? Where did I come from? How did I get here?

Now is the time to begin the education of that child. The answers it receives will in all probability be forgotten. But what is said to the child at this time will affect its character and influence its future. Untruth and deceit are as harmful to the character in the education of the child at this time as are drugs and poisons to an adult. Honesty and truthfulness are inherent. These virtues are to be drawn out and developed; they cannot be acquired. They should not be arrested, diverted or suppressed. The conscious something that has its temporary abode in that child is to be an inseparable portion of an intelligent Doer, the operator of the body, who is not born and cannot die with or after the death of its body. The duty of the Doer is to become conscious of itself and as itself while in the body and to re-establish its relation to the right thinking and all-knowing Triune Self of which it is an integral part. If the conscious portion of the Doer in the child becomes conscious *as* itself in the body and *of* its Triune Self, the Doer may eventually change its imperfect body into an undying body, such as the body it once did have. When the Doer finally changes the imperfect mortal body into an immortal perfect body, it will fit itself to be and it will be established as the conscious agent on earth of its all-knowing Triune Self in The Eternal. When this is done, the bridge will be established between The Eternal Order of Progression of The Realm of Permanence and this man-and-woman-world of change and birth and death.

When the conscious something is overcome by the body senses, and its body-mind is trained to dominate its feeling-mind and desire-mind, the body-mind and senses lull the conscious something into forgetfulness of itself, while it dreams the dream of the life of the senses until the body dies. So the conscious something in every man and every woman has been coming and going, life after life, without becoming conscious of the permanent reality of itself while in the temporary body which it takes on when it comes. It can dream through as many lives and wear out as many bodies as it will, but the inevitable destiny of the Doer is that it must, and in some one life it will, begin its real work of the ages: the building of the deathless, perfect physical body which, when completed, will be everlasting through all ages. And that body—"the second temple"—which it will build, will be greater than the body which it inherited and lost.

Well, if the mother's answers are harmful to her child, what then can she say that will help her child?

When John or Mary asks the mother the usual questions concerning its origin and identity, and where it came from, or how she got it, then the mother should draw the child to her and, giving it her entire attention, she should speak clearly and lovingly in her own affectionate way. Calling it by some such word as "Dear" or "Darling," she can say: "Now that you ask about yourself the time has come for us to talk about you and about your body. I will tell you what I can, and then you will tell me what you can; and perhaps you can tell me more about yourself than I know about you. You must already know, Dear, that the body you are in is not *you*, else you would not ask me who you are. Now I will tell you something about your body.

52

"You had to have a body to come into this world to meet Daddy and me, and to learn about the world and the people in the world. You could not grow a body for yourself, so Daddy and I had to get one for you. Daddy gave me a very tiny part of his body, and I took it with a tiny part in my body and these grew into one body. That little body had to be grown so carefully that I kept it inside my own body, close to my heart. I waited a long time until it had grown strong enough to come outside. Then one day when it was strong enough, the doctor came and took it out for me and put it into my arms. Oh! it was such a dear, wee little baby. It could not see or hear; it was too small to walk, and too small for you to come into then. It had to be cared for and fed, so that it would grow. I took care of it for you and trained it to see and hear and talk, so that it would be ready for you to see and hear when you were ready to come. I named the baby John (or Mary). I taught the baby how to speak; but it is not *you*. I have waited a long time for you to come, so that you could ask me about the baby which I have grown for you, and so that you could tell me about yourself. And now you are in the body, and you are going to live in that body with Daddy and me. While your body is growing, we are going to help you learn all about your body and about the world that you want to learn. But first, Dear, tell me: When did you find yourself in the body you are now in?"

This is the mother's first question to the conscious something in her child. It can be the beginning of the real education of that child.

Before the mother has put this question, the conscious something in the child may have asked to be told more about the baby body. If so, she can answer the questions as straightforwardly and simply as was her account of how she got the baby. But when she puts her question and other questions she will ask, she should clearly understand and keep in mind the following facts:

As the mother of her child, she is not speaking to *her* little child, the product of her body. She is questioning or speaking to the conscious something in that body.

The conscious something in her child is older than the ages; it is not conscious of time when not in the body, though it is limited by time and the senses of the body in which it is.

The conscious something is not physical; it is not a baby, a child, a human, though it makes the body into which it comes a human body.

When the conscious something comes into the body, it is at first concerned about itself, not about the body. Usually when it is conscious that those it asks about itself do not know, or tell it what it knows is not so, it will stop asking such questions. Then the parent may think it has forgotten; but it has not—not yet!

When it asks about itself, the conscious something should be addressed as itself.

It should be addressed as Welcome One, Conscious One, Friend, or by any other phrase or term that will distinguish it from the body; or it may be asked, and it may say, what it wishes to be called.

The conscious something is intelligent. It is as intelligent as the one who speaks to it, but it is limited by the undeveloped body, and by its unfamiliarity with the language and the words to express itself.

It is not conscious of the Triune Self to which it belongs, though it is a portion of one of the three inseparable parts of that Triune Self. These matters should be remembered when speaking to the conscious something about itself.

When the conscious something is in the child, and while it still asks who and what it is and where it comes from, it will, by its own thinking, either keep the way open for it to identify itself and be in phase with its own Thinker and Knower, or it will, by its thinking, put itself out of phase with these parts of its Triune Self, by identifying itself with the senses, and so it shuts itself in the body.

The conscious something cannot remain in the indeterminate state in which it is. By its thinking it will identify itself either with the Doer, of which it is a portion, or with the senses of the body and as the body.

When the conscious something first comes into the body, it is not enough conscious as itself to decide what it will think. The thinking of almost every conscious something will be guided and determined by the mother or guardians of the body into which it came.

If the conscious something is not helped in its thinking with its feeling-mind and desire-mind to become conscious as itself, or at least to keep on thinking of itself as *not* the body in which it is, it will eventually be shut in by the body-mind and by the four senses of the body; it will cease to be conscious as it now is and will identify itself as the body.

Then that conscious something will be as ignorant about itself as are all the other conscious somethings in the bodies of men and women in the world. They do not know what they are, who they are, where they came from, or how they got here; nor do they know what they will do after their bodies die.

One of the important facts to consider about the conscious something is that it has three minds—three ways of thinking which it may use: either to keep itself in ignorance of itself by thinking of itself as the body and the senses; or to find and free itself by seeing and knowing things as they are, and by doing with them what it knows should be done.

The body-mind of the conscious something cannot be used to tell it anything about itself; but it can be employed in using the senses to find the means to supply the cravings of the bodily appetites, feelings and desires; or it may be trained by the conscious something and it can train the senses to search into all the realms and forces and worlds of nature and do with them what that conscious something wills.

The feeling-mind can be led by the body-mind to feel all sensations of the senses and be controlled by them; or it may be trained by the conscious something to control and subordinate and be independent of the body, and "isolate" feeling from sensations and the body, and be itself free.

The desire-mind can be led by the body-mind to find ways and means of expressing through the senses the feelings and desires for nature; or it can be trained by the will to find and free the conscious something from its control by nature.

It is possible for the conscious something in a man body or a woman body to train the feeling-mind and desire-mind to control the body-mind, so that the body-mind will not be a hindrance to the conscious self in the finding of itself while still in the body, though there is no evidence in history that this has been done, and the information how to do it has not so far been made available.

Therefore, if the conscious something in the child is not to be put into the waking dream-sleep by the senses and its guardians and so made to forget itself and lose itself in the body, it must be kept conscious of itself in the body, and be helped to find what it is and where it came from, while it is still conscious that it is not the body and the senses.

Not every conscious something will wish to remain conscious of itself after it gets accustomed to the body it is in; many will wish to play the game of make-believe which they see men and women are playing. Then the conscious something will let the senses lull it to sleep and forget itself and dream itself through the partition of forgetfulness as a man or as a woman. Then it will not be able to remember the time when it was conscious of itself as not the child body in which it found itself. Then it will receive instructions of the senses and will, by the senses, memorize the instructions so received, and will have little or no information from the parts of itself not in the body.

In many instances, the conscious something in the child has striven stubbornly against being told that it was the body named John or Mary, and that it belonged to the mother and father. But without help it could not very long continue to remain conscious of itself while constantly being referred to as being the body; so eventually the senses of its developing body shut it in and it was made to forget itself and take as its identity the name given the body it is in.

Therefore, the conscious something in the body of man and of woman is shut off from communication with its other parts by the physiological disarrangements in the structural development of its body.

The channels for communication between the conscious something in the body and its parts not in the body are chiefly concerned with the development and relation between the ductless glands and the voluntary and the involuntary nervous systems.

If the conscious something in the child remains conscious of itself as being distinct and different from the physical body in which it is, its physiological development will be so accommodated to the conscious something that it will be provided with the necessary channels for communication with parts of itself not in the body.

Therefore, in answering the questions of her child, the mother should try to understand that if that conscious something is not helped by her thinking in her questions to have confidence in itself and to remain conscious as itself, that it will be shut in by the senses of its body and will forget itself—just as she has been shut in and has forgotten the time when her own conscious something asked questions of her mother similar to the questions which the conscious something in her child is now asking her.

If the conscious something were the body, it would have no doubt at all about it, and therefore would have no occasion to ask either itself or the mother. The reason why the conscious something asks, Who am I?, is that it has a permanent identity of which it is conscious and with which it wishes to be identified. It asks, Who am I?, in the hope that it will be told, just as one who has lost his way and forgotten his name asks to be reminded or told who he is.

Now, what happens to that conscious something after the mother has explained what the body is and how she got it, and has distinguished it from the child and told it she has been waiting for it and is glad it has come?

That conscious something should at once have reassured confidence in itself and feel safe with the friend-mother who is glad it has come to her. It is welcome. That gives it the best feeling and puts it in the best frame of mind it could be in at that time. That should make it feel somewhat like one who is on a visit in a strange country and is among friends. And then the mother asks: "When did you find yourself in the body you are now in?"

This question should produce an important effect on the conscious something and should call its powers into action. It is asked a question. The question requires it to remember itself as it was before it came into the body, and to remember when it entered the body. The conscious something has memory, but its memory is of itself and is in itself, of feeling or desire; it is not memory of any of the objects of the senses. To remember anything of itself it must think with the feeling-mind or with the desire-mind. The question requires it to first use its feeling-mind and desire-mind for itself, and to call to its assistance its body-mind, because the body-mind can only tell it when it entered the body. The body-mind is then called upon to reproduce the happenings or incidents connected with the entrance of that conscious something into the body. These incidents are of the objects or events recorded on the breath-form by one or more of the senses, and of which the breath-form bears the record.

The question: "When did you find yourself in the body you are now in?," may so stimulate the conscious something that it will operate each of its three minds. If so, it will distinguish itself from the body; with its desire-mind and feeling-mind it will require the body-mind to reproduce from the recorded memories the time of its entrance into the body. It is possible for it to get an insight why it lost its perfect body and became human. By doing this it would begin putting the three minds into their right relation with each other, which would subordinate the body-mind to the other two. The conscious self will tell the mother of John or Mary just what happened and just how it felt about what happened, and about itself when it came in; or it may be more or less confused, but it will reply in its own original and characteristic way if it is helped by the mother.

The next question which the mother should ask is: "Where did you come from?"

That is a difficult question to answer. It cannot be answered in terms of the senses, because the conscious something has come out of istence into existence, into a sense body, from itself in istence. But the conscious something—if the mother is in sympathy with it—will give an answer which it can give because it has its istence memory, memory of itself in itself; and its answer may be a revelation to the mother and an awakening of itself in its human dream-world.

The mother may then ask: "Tell me, Dear, did you come into your body to do some special thing, or did you come to learn about yourself and about the world? Whatever it is you came for, tell me and I will help you."

The question will elicit from the conscious something, or will remind it, of what its business or work in the world is to be. But its answer will not be clear, because it is not sufficiently acquainted with words and with the world to give a definite answer. The answer will itself suggest how it should be dealt with and the questions it should be asked.

If the conscious something should not give satisfactory answers, the answers should nevertheless be written down— all the questions and answers should be recorded. The mother should think about the questions and answers, and the questions should, with variations, be asked again and again, to keep the conscious something thinking about itself so that it may establish direct communication with itself and the other portions and parts not in the body.

The conscious something in the body is related to the Thinker of the Triune Self who is not in the body. It is from that Thinker that the conscious something may, through the channels it will provide, be self-taught, "God"-taught, by actual in-tuition. That teaching will be true; it will tell what things are as they are, instead of making the mistake now made by accepting things to be what the senses and the sense organs make them appear to be. The self-teaching will adjust and correct the senses and put to use all impressions that they bring in, giving to each impression its true value.

The results of such questioning are: by speaking to the conscious something simply and understandingly, the mother gains its confidence and gives it confidence in itself. By telling it she has expected it and has waited for it, she gives it a place in the family and a place in the world. By talking with it concerning what it is and where it came from, she helps to keep it conscious *of* and *as* itself and opens the way for it to get into communication with and get information from other parts not in the body. By helping it to continue to be conscious of itself as different from the body it is in, she makes it possible for it to be really educated, so that she and others may be educated; that is, that each one may draw out the knowledge from its own source of knowledge. By demonstrating through the conscious something that there is another and greater source of knowledge than that which can be acquired through the senses, that conscious something may be one of the first of the pioneers in establishing the new system of education which the world needs and must have, to prevent the breakdown of civilization. It is a system of education by which the present shut-ins may be shown the way and begin the process of opening the channels to their own sources of knowledge—the source of vast knowledge to which every individual human in the world is heir, even though he does not know it. The heritage is ready, when the heir is ready to receive the inheritance; that is, when the conscious something now shut in by the senses of the body will establish its right to inherit the knowledge. It proves its right by opening the lines of communication and relation with the Thinker and the Knower of the Triune Self to which it, the Doer, the conscious something, belongs.

Instead of telling the conscious something the names of the things of the senses, the questions of the mother will make it think—to think into itself first, and then to relate itself to the child body and to time and place. To do this it must think with its feeling-mind or desire-mind first; and then, when the feeling-mind and the desire-mind each has confidence in itself, with its body-mind. This is the beginning of the training of the feeling-mind or desire-mind and of their subordinating the body-mind. The feeling-mind is trained and developed by thinking of subjects, about feeling, what feeling is, how feeling operates in itself, and by creating mental images in imagination. The desire-mind is trained and developed by thinking about desire: what is desire, how does it operate, what is its relation to feeling; and to will, to create mental images from a point, in imagination, with feeling. The body-mind is trained and developed by thinking of objects and things of the senses in terms of size, figure, weight, and distance.

Every day, the Doer, each conscious something in thousands of children in the world, asks such questions: "Who am I?" "Where did I come from?" "How did I get here?" These or like questions are asked by the Doers, self-exiled from their immortal Triune Selves. They feel lost in an unknown world. As soon as they are sufficiently familiar with the bodies they are in and can use the words, they ask for information, for help. When the truly loving mothers and the really competent educators will and do realize these truths, they will give the information asked for and the help needed. If the mothers and educators will help the conscious something in the child to have confidence in itself and to keep the channels in its body clear and clean, some of the incoming Doers will prove the sources of knowledge at present unknown, and they may be the means of the inauguration of that knowledge into the world.

PART III

The Immortal and Inseparable Twain in Every Human Being

There was a time in the unwritten history of the immortal Doer in every human body—truer than any human history—when as a twain it lived in a perfect sexless body, in The Realm of Permanence, which is usually spoken of as Paradise or the Garden of Eden, in the interior of the earth. The Doer of the Triune Self was conscious of itself as the twain, and as *not* the body *in* which it lived. It was just as sure that the body was *not itself* as the human is now sure it is not the clothes it wears. The body of the Doer had unfailing youth and strength and beauty imparted to it by itself as the twain, desire-and-feeling; and it was without pain or any of the ills and sorrows with which the human being now afflicts itself. And the Doer had power to see and hear in every part of the world, and to do as it willed. It was the "first temple," or body, spoken of in Masonry. And so the Doer saw and heard and did. (*See* chapter: The Perfect Sexless Immortal Physical Body)

In due course the desire of the Doer desired to see the feeling of itself expressed in a body apart from the body in which it, the Doer, dwelt. Likewise, feeling of the Doer felt the need to see the desire of itself expressed in a body and apart

63

from itself. And, as desire willed, there was breathed out from the body of the Doer a form into which, as though by extension from desire, feeling entered, by feeling itself into that form. So the Doer, by the extension of its body and extending a part of itself into the extension, lived in a double body, as the twain, the two bodies being united by bonds of attraction. This is the basis of the story of "Adam," and the "rib" out of which was fashioned "Eve."

Each of the two bodies was at first like the other because desire-and-feeling were one twain when the Doer extended the form; but, though each of the bodies bore a likeness to the other, each was different from the other. The likeness was caused by the one-ness and inseparability of desire-and-feeling. The difference was the result of the separation by extension, as two, into the double body. The single body had expressed the one-ness of desire-and-feeling, as one. The double body represented the one as two-ness, as desire and as feeling. The body in which was desire expressed power, in the strength of body; the body in which was feeling expressed beauty, through the form of body. So the structure and function of the body of desire were determined by the power as desire, and those of the body of feeling were formed to express beauty as feeling. And each of the bodies was in structure and function so formed as to relate to the other and to be the complement of the other, similarly as desire-and-feeling were related and complemented each in the other and by the other.

While desire-and-feeling were together one, they were conscious as one and acted as one. When one was an extension of the other they were still conscious as one, but in the double body they seemed to be two and acted as two. Desire acted more independently of feeling, and, likewise, feeling acted more independently of desire, although whatever each did was done with due regard to the other. Desire-and-feeling were conscious of their inseparability, but the more each in its body acted as though it were independent of the other, the more the bodies changed, until the twain body became two separate bodies. The matter of the twain body of the Doer had been so perfectly related and adapted to the twain that it at once expressed in form and function the character of desire-and-feeling. The separation of the twain body into two separate bodies was therefore due to desire and feeling, not to the double body.

Desire looked out from its body upon the body of feeling and electrified the parts of its body into activity while it looked upon that form of beauty. Feeling gazed through its body upon the body of desire and magnetized the parts of its body into passivity while it looked upon that body of strength. Thus each, looking upon the other through its own opposite and complementary body, fell under the spell of the senses. And the Doer was by its body-mind beguiled into thinking it was two. That is to say, desire-and-feeling were conscious as one and the same while they thought in themselves as desire-and-feeling; but while they looked through their bodily senses of sight, the body-mind through sight showed them that they were two, and different. Their thinking followed the senses and each so charged and changed its body that the body of each attracted and drew to itself the body of the other. By the prompting of the body-mind, desire desired to be in and one with feeling through the body of feeling, instead of having feeling in itself; and feeling felt to get and be one with desire with the body of desire, instead of having desire in itself. While the Doer thus looked out from itself onto the two bodies of itself, desire-and-feeling gradually changed the nature and the structure of its bodies—which were not sexual until after many changes they eventually became sexual bodies. By thus thinking, desire changed the structure and function of its body into a male body; and feeling changed the structure and function of its body into a female body. When not led into thinking passively through their bodily senses, and when thinking actively in themselves, desire-and-feeling knew that each was an inseparable part of the other, but when they looked through or thought with the body-mind through the senses, they were deceived by the body-mind into thinking passively through the senses of their bodies that they were their bodies. Thus, when the desire in the man body looked upon the woman body of feeling, it was by its male body-mind made to think that it was that man body and it desired union with the feeling of itself in the woman body; and, when feeling in the woman body looked upon the man body of desire, feeling was by its female body-mind made to think that it was that woman body and it craved union with the desire of itself in the man body. Each looking upon itself in the body of the other saw the reflection by extension of itself in that other body—like as in a mirror. So, instead of having union of its desire-and-feeling as one-ness in the perfect body, the Doer had its man body enter into and have union with the woman body. Through long periods of thinking, the structure of each body was changed.

Before the union of its two bodies, the Doer did not sleep. Sleep was not needed for the Doer in its perfect body or for either of its bodies. The bodies did not need sleep for rest or repair or refreshment, nor did they need human food, because they were maintained by breathing alone. The bodies did not cause the Doer to suffer; they were unaffected by time and were kept young and beautiful by desire-and-feeling. The Doer was continuously conscious of itself as desire-and-feeling under all conditions, in or without its bodies. Then the Doer could think of the differences of itself from its bodies. But after the union of bodies it could not so think. It could not think clearly or steadily, nor could it see or hear as it formerly had done. What had happened was that the Doer had allowed its body-mind to put it as feeling-and-desire into a self-hypnosis; it had hypnotized itself. This it had done by thinking of itself as the senses had led it to think; that is, to think with the body-mind that it as desire was the physical body, and that it as feeling was the physical body in which feeling was. By so continuing to think, desire-and-feeling imparted its active and its passive powers to the units of the physical bodies, and so unbalanced and charged the two bodies that each attracted the other until the bodies had sexual union. Thus the bodies completed the self-hypnosis which the Doer had put itself into. Sexual union was the "original sin."

By its desiring and feeling and thinking union of the man and woman bodies, the Doer had drawn together and concentrated the elemental nature forces of fire and air and water and earth. By thinking, desire and feeling were focussed with those elemental forces and were, so to say, attached and wedded to their physical bodies. During the union a light of the eyes of each of the bodies was transferred to their sexual organs; so the eyes were dimmed and the hearing deadened. The Doer's perceptions through the senses were limited to impressions on the organs and nerves of the physical senses. The Doer had put itself to sleep; and it dreamed, of sensations.

Formerly the Doer had not depended on the senses to tell it what it should think or what it should do. Before the Doer had desired union of bodies it was in direct relation with the Thinker, that is, with rightness, its law, and with reason, its judge. Then reason tutored desire, and rightness inspired feeling in all their thinking and in all their acts. Then desire-and-feeling were together one Doer. The Doer had no preferences for some things, nor prejudices against other things. It was not in doubt about anything, because where rightness and reason are, doubt cannot be. But now that desire-and-feeling of the Doer had made themselves appear to be divided and separated from each other by the man and woman bodies, there was doubt, which is indecision in distinguishing sense from reason. Doubt caused division, as it were, in desire. Desire, on the one hand, desired Self-knowledge and desired reason to guide it. Desire, on the other hand, desired sexual union and allowed the bodily senses to lead it. The desire for the sexes rebelled against the desire for Self-knowledge, but could not control or change it. And the desire for the sexes had eventuated in union of the man and woman bodies. Desire for the sexes divorced itself from the desire for Self-knowledge, and so from rightness and reason. Desire-and-feeling were conscious of wrong, and they suffered. They were in fear. Instead of thinking and desiring for their rightness and reason to enlighten and direct them, the desire-and-feeling for the sexes turned from the Conscious Light, which is Truth, and which comes through rightness and reason. Without the Conscious Light, Truth, desire-and-feeling allowed the body-mind to identify them with the senses of seeing and hearing and tasting and smelling, which cannot tell what things really are. So the thinking and actions of desire-and-feeling were impelled by the promptings of the senses of the man and woman bodies, in which they wished to be hidden from their own rightness and reason.

As the Doer had divorced itself from its Triune Self, of which it still was nevertheless a part, and had attached itself to nature, it made itself dependent for guidance on the four senses. Without desire-and-feeling the body and its senses would be at a standstill, inert. But with desire-and-feeling and their power to think, they could produce phenomena of nature. The immortal twain identified itself with the man and woman bodies, and the four senses became its representatives and guides. All that the twain desired and felt and hoped to be was interpreted by it in terms of the four senses. Its desires multiplied; but, however many, all had to come under the generalship of four desires: the desire for food, the desire for possessions, the desire for a name, and the desire for power. These four desires were related to the four senses, and the four senses represented and guided the four systems of the body. The four senses of seeing and hearing and tasting and smelling were the channels through which the radiant and airy and fluid and solid matter flowed into and out of the generative and respiratory and circulatory and digestive systems. And the four general desires of the desire for the sexes, thus harnessed into and geared to systems and senses and states of matter and elements of nature, kept the body-machines going and, likewise, helped to keep the nature-machine of the man-and-woman-world in operation. The Doer continued, as it were, to personify the body and the four senses. It continued to relate itself to the things of the senses until it could not think of its desire-and-feeling as being distinct from the body and the senses. But the desire for Self-knowledge was never changed. It will not be satisfied until the Doer accomplishes the real union of desire-and-feeling.

The perfect body of the twain was not born, it did not die. It was a body of Permanence, a body of compositor units which were balanced, not male or female; that is, what had been the active and passive sides of the unit were equalized; neither side could control its other side, and all the units were balanced, complete, in harmony with The Realm of Permanence, and therefore not subject to growth and decay and the wars and re-adjustments in this physical world of change. The bodies of man and woman are in a continual process of growth and decay from birth to death. The bodies eat and drink and are entirely dependent on nature for the maintenance of their broken, incomplete, and temporary structures, and they are out of tune with The Realm of Permanence.

The perfect body, the "first temple," in The Realm of Permanence, was a body with two spinal columns, in perfect accord with the four worlds of nature through the four senses and their systems. The front column was the nature column, in which were four stations for communication with nature by means of the involuntary nervous system. Through the front spinal column, eternal life was imparted to the body from the immortal twain. The rear spinal column was the column of the Doer, the column through which the twain could operate with nature and for nature by means of the voluntary nervous system, through the four senses. From its rear spinal column and through the four senses, the Doer could see and hear and taste and smell any object or thing in any state of matter in any division of the physical world or form world. The duty of the Doer was to use the permanent body as a perfect machine with the four senses and their systems as instruments, for the sensing and operation of the units making up the great nature-machine.

At this point in its course, the Doer had a duty to perform and a destiny to fulfill. Its destiny was that its desire-and-feeling be in permanently balanced union, so that it would be perfectly related to the otherwise perfect Triune Self, of which it was an integral part; and so that it could be one of those who guide the operations of nature in relation to the affairs of mankind. Desire-and-feeling in such permanently balanced union could not then in any way become attached to or affected by nature.

While the twain had dwelt in its body of Permanence, it was conscious of its Thinker and of its Knower, and its thinking was in accord with their thinking. By effecting the union of its desire-and-feeling, the twain would be a qualified officer of nature for the perpetuation of law and justice in the physical and form worlds. Desire-and-feeling did not then see and hear and taste and smell after the manner of human beings. These were the instrumental functions of nature units, as senses. Desire was conscious power; it functioned as I am, I will, I do, I have; its functions were to change itself, and to empower nature units to action and to progress. Feeling was conscious beauty, and it functioned as perceptiveness, conceptiveness, formativeness, and projectiveness. Desire-and-feeling were conscious of the objects and doings of nature by means of the senses, and they were to deal with objects and events according to the dictates of law and justice. To be competent to act in harmony with law and in compliance with justice, it was necessary that desire-and-feeling be immune from the allurements or temptations of the senses and to be unattached to the objects of nature.

While desire-and-feeling had been in direct relation with the law and justice of rightness and reason, they could not do wrong or act unjustly. The rightness of law and the justice of reason were in perfect harmony, in union. They needed no perfecting; they were perfect. Under their direction, desire-and-feeling would think in accord with their thinking. Desire-and-feeling could not in this way again be of themselves immune to the things of the senses. To be immune, it was necessary that desire-and-feeling be tried and, of their own free will, proven immune, in the balances of nature; that is, in a man body and a woman body. The balancing must be done with separate bodies. Through the perfect body the twain had observed the perfected Triune Selves working with the nature beings in the light world and life world and form world with relation to human beings in the physical world. But the twain had merely observed. It had taken no part in such work because it was not yet a duly qualified and constituted officer of law and justice. It had observed the coursings of the nature units in their comings and goings, and it had observed the administration of justice to the desire-and-feeling in human beings in servitude to sensation. It was conscious that the attachment of the Doers to the things of the senses and their ignorance about themselves are the causes of the slavery of human beings. The twain, merely observing, did not try to think, and it did not try to judge. But it was with rightness and reason, and it was informed by them concerning nature and about the causes and their results concerning human beings and human destiny. The Doer, being thus advised, was left free to decide what it willed not to do and what it willed to do. The Doer willed; that is to say, it desired. Desire willed to see feeling in a form apart from the body in which it was.

In the course of events, the perfect body of the Doer was changed until it had separated into a male body and a female body. It had been made invulnerable to all forces and powers, except to the power of the Doer. By thinking, desire-and-feel-

71

ing could and did change the units of their bodies into active-passive and passive-active, but they could not destroy the units.

According to the plan and purpose of the test, this was as far as the Doer should have gone in its change of the units of the perfect body. To go further would defeat the purpose in the changing of the one body in which the units were in perfect balance, into the male and the female bodies. These two bodies were figuratively, so to say, the bodies as balances, by which inseparable desire-and-feeling were to be adjusted to each other until they were balanced. The standards of balancing were reason and rightness. Desire-and-feeling were to do the balancing. Desire was to be in accord with reason by thinking and desiring itself into accord. Feeling was to be in agreement with rightness by thinking and feeling itself into agreement with rightness. When desire-and-feeling, the Doer, by their thinking with reason-and-rightness, had come into perfect relation with the Thinker of the Triune Self, they would by so doing be at once in right relation with each other, in union, and permanently balanced. The two bodies, as scales, were to be the means of effecting such a balance and permanent union. The union was not to be of the two bodies as one, because they were the scales and should remain two until desire-and-feeling had each desired and felt in balance with reason-and-rightness. Thus in balance, they would be balanced in complete union. Then it would have been impossible for feeling-and-desire to be deluded into believing they were two bodies, because in reality they were one and their thinking with rightness-and-reason had made them conscious as one, the Doer. As the one body had been divided as two, so the two were to be again united as one. And the two, again one, could nevermore separate, because the Doer in the then immortal body would be one, and conscious as one with the Thinker and with the Knower as the Triune Self. Thus the Doer would be the agent of the

Triune Self and would be one of the administrators of destiny for nature and for mankind.

That would have been according to plan and purpose and would have been the result if desire-and-feeling had trained their own desire-mind and feeling-mind to think according to rightness and reason. On the contrary, they were led by the senses to think with the body-mind. The body-mind was to be used by the Doer in thinking for nature, but not until after desire-and-feeling had first learned to control and use their own minds. As the Doer, they had observed other Doers. The Thinker had made plain that they should control their own desire-mind and feeling-mind by thinking for union with each other, and that after their union they were to think with the body-mind for nature. The Doer had observed that the condition of the Doers in human bodies was the result of their thinking with the body-mind, and it had been warned that such would be the destiny it would make for itself if it should do likewise.

The thinking of desire would have led it to the knowledge of itself as desire, and the thinking of feeling would have led it to the knowledge of itself as feeling. Such thinking would have balanced and also would have enabled them, as the Doer, to think with the body-mind without identifying itself with the senses and as the body. Instead, by their thinking with the body-mind, they hypnotized themselves by thinking of themselves as their bodies, and thereby desire-and-feeling identified themselves with and as the sensations in those bodies. This condition could not have been brought about in any other way than by thinking with the body-mind for the body.

Thus the Doer brought about the division and separation of the once-perfect body into two imperfect bodies. The body in which desire was, retained the form of the rear spinal column unbroken, though the structures of the lower part grew together, and the lower—now called the terminal filament—and the body lost the strength it once had had. The body in

73

which feeling was, retained only a remnant of its broken front column. The sternum is the remnant, with bare cartilaginous vestiges of the once articulated front column. The loss of one of the two columns disorganized and weakened the structure and deformed both bodies. Then each of the two bodies had a rear spinal column but not a front spinal column. Both bodies were further deformed and limited in their functions by the transformation of the front column and cord into the digestive system with its nerve structures, which included the vagus nerve of the voluntary nervous system. The front spinal cord was the conductor of eternal life and youth which the twain gave to the body while the body was one.

The two-columned body did not need for its maintenance the food which the human now consumes, because that body was self-perpetuating through the breath and did not die. It was a body composed of units in stages of progression. Death had no power over the units because they were balanced, poised, and immune from disease, decay and death. The units were complete; the body was complete; the body of units was a body of Permanence. The only power which could either interrupt or continue the progress of the units was the power of desire-and-feeling, the Doer. That is to say, if the twain so willed, by thinking it would be united in inseparable union, unaffected by the senses—it would be free. So thinking and acting, the Doer would keep the units of its body in their order of progression. But the Doer in the man or woman body of today did not take that course of thinking and acting. It let its thinking be controlled by the senses of the man and woman bodies into which were divided the units of its permanent body. And by thinking of itself as two, the balanced units of its permanent body were thrown out of balance. The units were then subject to change, and the bodies required food for the maintenance of the changes until they were interrupted by death.

74

The unbalanced units of the body act as active-passive in a man body and as passive-active in a woman body. To so act, the front spinal column and its cord, which conducted the Light from the twain down the front cord and up the rear spinal cord back to the head, and which gave life to the perfect body, were transformed into the alimentary canal and the involuntary nervous system, joined by the vagus nerve. Now, food holding Light and life must pass through this canal so that the blood may extract from the food the materials needed for the upkeep of the body. Thus, instead of having its Light from desire-and-feeling, the body now depends for its life on food from nature which must pass through the alimentary canal, this being a part of the reconstructed spinal cord of the former front column.

Because of its wrong thinking, the twain destined the compositor units to leave the transient units of its body to disperse and, after a while, to recompose other transient units into another living body; that is, to live and to die, to live again and again to die, each life followed by death and each death followed by another life; and it destined itself to re-exist in each new life, in a man body or in a woman body. And because the body had been made subject to death through sexual union, so also it must now be restored to life through sexual union in order that, as desire or as feeling, it might re-exist.

The Doer cannot cease to be. It is immortal, but it is not free; it is responsible for the units of its once perfect body—they cannot cease to be. The Doer will inevitably redeem itself from nature and will have union of its desire-and-feeling; it will balance and re-establish the compositor units as the perfect and permanent body for the uninterrupted progression of nature, which they are.

Since its first existence, and after the death and dissolution of that body, the inseparable twain has periodically re-existed. In each re-existence, desire-and-feeling are together. The twain does not re-exist in a man body and in a woman body at the same time. Desire-and-feeling, always together, re-exist in one man body or in one woman body. In the natural man body there is the twain, but desire dominates feeling and feeling is subordinate to desire. In the normal woman body, feeling prevails over desire and desire is in abeyance to feeling. The periodical re-existences continue, but they cannot always continue. Soon or late, every Doer must do its duty and work out its destiny. It will, from inevitable necessity, awake from and take itself out of its hypnosis and will free itself from bondage to nature. It will in the future do what it should have done in the past. There will be a time when the inseparable twain will be conscious that it is in dream, and will discover itself as *not* the body in which it dreams. Then, by its efforts to think of itself as itself, it will distinguish itself to be different and distinct from the body in which it is. The Doer will, by thinking, first isolate its feeling and later isolate its desire. Then it will bring these into conscious and inseparable union. They will be in everlasting love. Then, not before, will they really know love. The Doer will then put itself into conscious relation with the Thinker and Knower of the immortal and self-knowing Triune Self. As the Doer of the Triune Self it will be in right relation with rightness-and-reason, as the Thinker; and with identity-and-knowledge, as the Knower of the Triune Self. Then it will be one among the intelligent Triune Selves who guard and guide the destinies which the sleeping Doers in human bodies make for themselves, while these continue to sleep on and to dream over and over again the lives of human beings, through life and through death, and from death again to life.

Such is the history and the destiny of every immortal twain in a human body which, thinking as desire, makes the human male a man, and which, thinking as feeling, makes the human female a woman.

⤜⤜⤜⤜⤜⤜⤜⤜⤜⤜⤜⤜⤜⤜⤜⤜⤜⤜⤜⤜⤜⤜⤜⤜⤜⤜⤜⤜⤜⤜⤜⤜⤜⤜

PART IV

MILESTONES ON THE GREAT WAY
TO CONSCIOUS IMMORTALITY

"KNOW THYSELF": The Finding and Freeing of the Conscious Self in the Body

As a guide for an understanding of the operation of nature, let it be repeated that the entire nature machine of the human world is composed of unintelligent units, which are conscious *as* their functions only. In developing, they progress by slow, very slow degrees from the least transient unit in the structure of nature to the most progressed in a human body; the most progressed is the breath-form unit, commonly called the subconscious mind, which has passed through all lesser degrees of development and is eventually the automatic, coordinating, formative, general manager of the entire human body; it is in and through its senses, systems, organs, cells and their constituents.

Each man or woman body is, so to say, a diminutive living model machine, according to which the entire nature machine of the human world is constructed. Following the patterns of the units of the human body, the units of nature are unbalanced, that is, either active-passive as in the male or passive-active as in the female.

Four lights of nature are necessary for the operation of nature: starlight, sunlight, moonlight, and earthlight. But these four lights are only reflections in nature, so to say, of the Conscious Light which is present in the human body. Without the Conscious Light from the human, nature could not function. Therefore, there is a constant pull by nature for the Conscious Light.

The pull of nature for Light in the human is exercised by the four senses. They are the ambassadors from nature to the Court of Man. The eyes, ears, mouth, and nose are the organs by means of which the senses and their nerves receive impressions from nature and send back the Light for which nature pulls. The operating procedure is: by the involuntary nerves of the sense organs, the objects of nature pull on the breath-form, which is centered in the front part of the pituitary body in the socket of the top of the sphenoid bone, nearly in the center of the skull.

Then the body-mind, thinking through the senses in the breath-form in response to the pull, draws Light from its feeling-desire, which is centered in the rear part of the pituitary body. And feeling-desire gives the Light because it is hypnotized and controlled by the body-mind, which thinks for nature only. Thus controlled by its body-mind, the Doer in the human is unable to distinguish itself from the four senses in the body. The Conscious Light comes from the Triune Self to its Doer part, feeling-desire, in the body. The Light comes through the top of the skull into the arachnoidal spaces within the skull cavity and into the ventricles of the brain. The third ventricle extends in front as a narrow channel into the stem of the pituitary, and the pineal body automatically directs the Light through that channel into the rear part of the pituitary, to be used by feeling-desire as required.

Feeling and desire are separated in the body in their fields of operation—feeling being in the nerves and desire in the blood. But their governing seat and center is in the rear part of the pituitary.

The fourfold pull of nature to get Light from the human for the maintenance of the functions of nature is exercised through the eyes and the sense of sight on the generative system, through the ears and the sense of hearing on the respiratory system, through the tongue and the sense of taste on the circulatory system, and through the nose and the sense of smell on the digestive system. The functioning of the organs and senses is carried on by the breath-form, which is the coordinator and operator of the involuntary nervous system in the body. But nature cannot get Light except by the passive or active thinking of feeling-and-desire. Therefore, the Light must come from feeling-and-desire by the thinking of the body-mind.

Thus, during all waking or dreaming hours, the body-mind, so to say, reaches over from the rear part to the front part of the pituitary body to think according to the senses for the maintenance of male and female nature. The physical evidences of these statements can be found in textbooks.

Biological and anatomical textbooks show that the fertilized ovum becomes an embryo; that the embryo becomes a fetus; that the fetus becomes an infant which develops into a man or a woman; and, that the man or woman body dies and disappears from this world.

Actually, hundreds of infants are born into this world every hour, and during the same hour hundreds of men and women die and leave the world without appearing to affect or interfere much with people of the world, except those who are concerned with the coming of the infants and the disposal of the dead bodies.

Each of these changes and developments is a miracle, a wonder, a marvel; an event which happens and is witnessed, but which is beyond our understanding; it transcends our immediate knowledge. It is! And the miracle gradually becomes of such common occurrence, and people become so accustomed to each event, that we let it happen and go about our business until birth and death compel us to pause, to inquire, and sometimes actually to think. We must think—if we ever are to know. And we can know. But we never will know about the miracles preceding births and following deaths unless we have information concerning the causes of births and deaths. There is a moving population in the world. In the long run, there is for every birth a death, and for every death a birth, regardless of periodical increases or decreases in population; a human body must be furnished for each conscious self to re-exist.

In every human body the cause of birth is the desire for the sexual act, the "original sin." The dominant desire for sex must choose to change itself. When, by persistent steady thinking with the Conscious Light within, and because the sexual act is the cause of death, the desire for sex becomes conscious that it never can be satisfied, it will choose to be at one with one's own desire for self-knowledge. It will eventually sublimate and regenerate and transform the present human body, to be the perfect sexless physical body for its Triune Self, and be in The Realm of Permanence.

The secret of birth and life and death is locked up in every man body and every woman body. Each human body contains the secret; the body is the lock. Every human being possesses the key to open the lock and make use of the secret of immortal youth—else it must continue to suffer death. The key is the conscious self in the human body. Each self must think and locate itself as the key—to open and explore the human body and know itself as itself while living in the body. Then, if it will, it can regenerate, and sublimate and transform its body to become a perfect sexless body of immortal life.

In order to find the conscious self and understand the method by which the foregoing statements can be followed, a plan is here given. One can easily verify what is said about the physical body. But no textbook deals with the conscious self, or with the forces that operate the body.

Seeing that one's conscious self in the physical body does not know who or what or where it is, how is it to be explained that the body is managed during waking and sleeping hours, or how it goes to sleep, or how it wakes up, or how it performs its activities such as digestion and absorption of food, or how it sees, hears, tastes, and smells; or how the self governs its speech and acts in the performance of the multitude of duties of life? All of these actions of the world and its people can be epitomized and told by understanding how a human body is constituted and how its functions are maintained.

By way of comparison, let one understand that a human body in its entirety is a microscopic model of the world and the surrounding universe; and that the functional activities in the body are necessary to the universe around it. For example, the material taken into the body as food serves not only for rebuilding the structure of the body, but while passing through the body the food is itself so acted on by the conscious self, that on its return to nature, the material takes some part in rebuilding the structure of the world by the presence of the intelligent Conscious Light that has been imparted to it by contact with the Self.

In the original perfect, sexless body—the first temple— there was, before the legendary "fall of man," a "cord" of what is now the involuntary nervous system of nature, within a flexible spinal column in front of the body from the pelvis to and connecting with what is now the sternum. The part now missing was the "rib" of the Bible story of Adam, out of which was fashioned the body of "Eve," his twain. (*See* chapter: "THE STORY OF ADAM AND EVE: The Story of Every Human Being")

The original perfect body, from which the imperfect human body has descended, was a two-columned body, the cords within the columns connecting with each other in the pelvis. Originally there was thus a front-spinal column and cord for the operation and activities of unintelligent nature through the involuntary nervous system, directed and observed by the conscious self in the voluntary nervous system. Only a remnant of the front column for nature now remains as the sternum in the human body; the "cord" of the front column is now widely distributed as dense networks of nerve fibres and plexuses over the internal organs within the trunk of the body. The nerve branches and fibres now arise from two cords which, issuing from the brain, are placed one on the right side and the other on the left side of the spinal column in the chest and the abdominal cavity. Within the present-day spinal column is the spinal cord for the activities of the conscious self.

From the mid-brain (mesencephalon) of the human, there are developed four little bulges (corpora quadrigemina) which receive varied sensory impressions and which determine the motor actions of the whole body. Certain nerve paths lead from these bulges to the spinal cord and enable the mid-brain to control the motor centers of the trunk and limbs. On either side of the mid-brain there is a group of cells, spoken of as the "red nucleus." When an impulse passes out of the mid-brain to excite some movement of the body, the red nucleus is the link, the switchboard, which establishes the connection between the mid-brain and the centers of the motor nerves in the spinal cord. Every movement of the body is operated by way of the switchboard, the red nucleus, which is to the right and the left of the median line in the brain, and is under the guidance of the Conscious Light. This wonder is certain and sure.

The practical application of the foregoing is that, while one is awake, all impressions affecting the body through the senses and the skin are received by the breath-form in the front part of the pituitary body; and that at the same moment the body-mind, thinking through the senses in the breath-form, so affects the conscious self, the Doer, feeling-desire, in the rear part of the pituitary body, that feeling-desire thinks according to the senses. That thinking calls for Conscious Light, which is automatically directed by the pineal body from the third ventricle to the conscious self.

The thinking by the body-mind attaches Conscious Light to the objects thought of. That Light, usually referred to as the intelligence in nature, shows the units how to build up the structure in the department of nature which corresponds to the part of the body in which those units received the Light. Thus the units composing the body, as well as the masses of units that merely pass through the body, bear the Light attached to them by thinking. And that same attached Light goes out and returns again and is reclaimed again and again until the conscious self in the body frees the Light by making it unattachable. Then the unattachable Light remains in the noetic atmosphere and is always available as knowledge to the conscious self in the body.

The Light sent out by thinking bears the stamp of the one who thinks, and however much it mingles with the Light of others, it will always return to the one who sent it out—as money going to a foreign country will return to the government that issued it.

The knowledge acquired by thinking through the senses is sense-knowledge; it changes as the senses change. Real knowledge is knowledge of the self. It is the Light itself; it does not change; it shows things as they really are, and not only as the senses make them appear to be. Sense-knowledge must of necessity always be of nature because the body-mind cannot think of anything that is not of nature. That is why the knowledge of all human beings is limited to everchanging nature.

When the feeling-mind suppresses the body-mind by regularly thinking of itself as feeling, until it feels itself as feeling inside the body and, later on, detaches, isolates itself from the body, then feeling will know itself as feeling; and, with desire, will control the body-mind. Then feeling-desire, with real knowledge of itself, will see and understand nature as the Conscious Light shows it to be. Feeling-desire will know itself as it is, and will know that all nature units of its physical body should be balanced and restored to The Eternal Order of Progression, instead of being retarded in rounds of circulation by the human beings in this world of change.

Thus feeling-and-desire in thinking gives Conscious Light to its body-mind, which thereby becomes attached and binds itself to objects of nature and becomes their slave. To be free from its bonds, it must free itself from the things to which it is bound.

Those who hunger and yearn for freedom from their slavery to the body and who will think and act to be free, will receive the Light to show them how to defeat death and live forever.

The conscious self in the body can be found and known by an almost unbelievably simple method, namely, by a persistent, systematic manner of breathing, and of feeling and thinking, which is described in detail in the chapters on "RE-GENERATION." This method can, in the future, be immeasurably aided if and when the individual as a child will have been systematically instructed at the mother's knee on how to revive its memory of "where it came from," and which is shown in Parts I and II of this book.

Corporeal, sensuous terms must from very necessity be used to describe being and beings for which there are at present no fitting or suitable terms. When the beings spoken of in this book become familiar to readers, better and more explicit or descriptive terms will be found or coined.

The perfect body here spoken of is complete; it does not depend on human food and drink; nothing can be added to it; nothing can be taken from it; it cannot be improved; it is a body sufficient in itself: complete and perfect. (*See* chapter: "The Perfect Sexless Immortal Physical Body")

The form of that perfect body is graven on the breath-form of each human being, and the rebuilding of the human body will begin when the human being stops thinking of or letting the thoughts of sex enter or in any way arouse and affect the desire for sex or lead to the act of sex. Sexual thoughts and acts cause death of the body. This must be so because such thinking or thought of the sexes causes the breath-form to change the germ cells or seed of the body to become male or female sex cells. The age of the body is not the most important consideration in effecting its regeneration. So long as the human can breathe properly and can think and feel as he should, it is possible for one to begin regeneration or reconstruction of the sexual body into a sexless body of everlasting life. And if one does not succeed in the present life, he continues in the next life or lives on earth, until he has an immortal physical body. The outer form and the structure of the body are known, the paths of the nerves have been indicated, and the relations between the motor nerves of the conscious self and the sensory nerves of nature that have to do with this transformation have been shown in this book.

An objection to the facts previously stated may be: If feeling-desire is the conscious self *in* the body but not *of* the body, it should know itself to be itself and not the body, just as one knows that the body is not the clothes one wears, and it should be able to distinguish itself from the body as the body is distinguished from the clothes.

If previous statements have not been understood, this is a reasonable objection. It is answered by the following self-evident facts: Apart from the self, the body has no identity, because the body as a whole is not conscious of itself as a body at any time. The body changes from infancy to age, whereas the conscious self is the self-same conscious self from its earliest memory to old age of the body, and during all that time it has not in any way changed. Feeling-and-desire can be conscious of the body and its parts can be sensed at any time, but feeling-and-desire as the conscious self is not physical. It cannot be sensed by anything other than by the self in the body.

Feeling must find itself and thereby know itself by isolating, detaching, itself from the senses. Each conscious self must do this for itself. It must begin by reasoning. Feeling must do it by thinking of itself as feeling only. Let feeling suppress all functions of the body-mind. This it can do by thinking of itself only. When it thinks *of* and is conscious *as* feeling only, it is in illumination, illuminated *as* Conscious Bliss, in the Conscious Light. Then the body-mind is tamed. Never again will feeling be hypnotized. Feeling knows itself.

By understanding the foregoing as a background for thinking, let one who seeks self-knowledge de-hypnotize himself by persistent efforts of feeling to think of itself only, until the body-mind is suppressed and feeling is isolated, detached, and is by itself known to be what it is. Then let feeling proceed to have desire free itself.

As feeling could not have been freed without assistance of desire, likewise desire must have the help of feeling in order to be itself detached from nature. Through innumerable lives, desire has bound itself to objects of the senses. Now that feeling is free, desire must also free itself. No power other than itself can free it. By its own power, and by its body-mind that deluded it, and the feeling-mind to make relation with the objects, it begins to detach itself. It would be impossible for desire to detach itself from the particular and numberless objects of the senses. But as all things are related to nature through the four senses, desire takes them in their order: food, possessions, fame, and power.

Beginning with the gross appetite for food, ranging from the satisfaction of hunger to gluttony and the delicacies of the epicure, desire examines with the Light which convinces it to relinquish without longing or regret all foods, except what is needed for the body's welfare. Then desire is freed from the slavery to food.

Next in order is desire for possessions—houses, clothes, lands, money. Under the Light all possessions—except such as are needed to maintain the body in health and condition commensurate with one's position and duties in life—without hesitation or doubt, desire lets go. It has overcome desire for possessions, which then are seen as snares, cares, and troubles. Desire is unattached to what it has.

Then desire for a name as fame is before it, such as reputation in finance or place in government, and fame as glory of outstanding achievement in any field of action. And the Light shows that all—except such as are duties, to be done without hope of praise or fear of blame—all are like chains to bind. Then desire lets go, and the chains fall away.

Then appears the subtlest of the four desires, the desire for power. Desire for power may assume appearance of the Big Boss, the Great Man, or any envied position or silent power. When one will act in positions of power from a sense of duty, no matter whether it brings glory or condemnation, and without complaint, he has mastered the desire for power.

Mastery of the four desire generals exposes the desire which stands behind and is that for which the four desire generals strive—the desire for sex. It may be in the lower walks of life or in the foremost ranks of men, but it is there, in whatever guise. It hides behind every crown, within common suit or ermine robe, in palace or in humble cottage. And when this chiefest test is seen, it is discovered to be—selfishness grounded in ignorance of itself. It is selfishness, because when all other desires are mastered and disappear, and all else in life is vain and empty, then love is believed to be the refuge and retreat.

Love of sex is selfish because it would bind to oneself another self, and oneself to that other. This might be well for the human, but it is bondage for one who seeks freedom from birth and death. Such love would be ignorant, because the unknown love within is mistakenly betrayed for the reflected love in the body of the other self, and because human sexual love is the cause of birth and death. Human love, however beautiful for the ignorant human, is nevertheless bondage to nature. For one who seeks self-knowledge, true love is to find and have union of feeling-desire within one's own body. This, desire knows, and is shown by the Conscious Light within, to be on the way to union with its twain, feeling. This will be the first step toward knowledge of, and union with, its Triune Self. Under the Conscious Light within, desire abolishes selfishness grounded in ignorance of itself and is in agreement with its unchangeable desire for self-knowledge. Then there is true marriage or union of feeling-desire in the physical body— which has been prepared and made ready by thinking for the work to this end—self-knowledge.

SELF-DE-HYPNOTIZATION:
A Step to Self-Knowledge

No hypnotized person knows that he is hypnotized. Furthermore, one who does not know *what* he or she is, *is* hypnotized. You are hypnotized, self-hypnotized, because you as a conscious self do not feel yourself in the body as distinctly as you feel the body to be distinct from the clothes it wears. Now, since you are self-hypnotized, you can de-hypnotize yourself, and then you will know yourself while in the physical body.

The facts are: You do not understand yourself to be distinct and different from the physical body in which you live. You do not know *who* or *what* you are—awake or asleep. When you are asked: Who are you?, you give the name which the parents had given to the body in which you live. But your body is not, cannot be, *you*. Scientists have declared that within every seven years the human body is entirely changed. Whereas, *you* are now the self-same identical "I," the conscious self, that you were when you first entered your constantly changing body. That is astonishing!

Let us consider a few commonplace matters: Do you know how you go to sleep? When you dream, is your identity the same as when you are awake? Where are *you* during deep sleep? You do not know what or where *you* are when not in the body; but certainly *you* cannot be the body, because the body rests in bed; it is dead to the world; it is not conscious of its parts, or of you, or of anything; the body is a mass of particles of constantly changing physical matter. On awakening, and while you are getting into touch with the body, before you are "awake," you sometimes wonder for a moment who and what and where you are. And, while you are getting into connection with the body, you may mentally say, if you live in a male body: "Oh, yes, I know. I am John Smith. I have an appointment and must get up." Or, if you live in a female body, you may say: "I am Betty Brown. I must dress myself and see about the house." Then you go on, and continue the life of yesterday. This is your common experience.

Thus throughout life you identify your own constant identity with the name given the infant body in which *you* took residence when it was ready for *you* to move in, some few years after its birth. At or about that time you became conscious of yourself in the body; *that* was your first memory. You could then begin to ask questions about yourself, about your body, and about people and the things in this world.

The process of de-hypnotizing oneself must of necessity begin with an attempt at self-analysis. You can question yourself: Of all things that I am conscious of, what do I really know? The right answer is: Of all the things of which I am conscious, there is only one thing that I really do know, and that is: *I am conscious.*

No human being really knows more about his conscious· self than just that. Why not? Because, as a basic fact, one knows without thinking that he is conscious, and there is no question or doubt about it. About every other thing there may be a doubt, or one has to think about what he is conscious of. But one does not have to think about the fact that he is conscious because there is no doubt about it.

There is one and only one other thing that one can know, but he must think about it. That fact is: I am conscious that I am conscious. Only a human being can really know that he is conscious. These two facts are all that anyone really knows about his conscious self.

90

By taking the next step toward self-knowledge, one begins to de-hypnotize himself. That is done when one asks and answers this question: *What* is it that is conscious, and is conscious that it is conscious?

When one is told what he is, he can assent and believe that. But mere belief is not self-knowledge. To really know oneself, the human being must and will by thinking persistently know by degrees what he is, however long it may take, until eventually he answers his question of *what* he really is. And that first step toward self-knowledge is so different from and superior to what he had only believed, that he will not be satisfied until he has taken all the steps or degrees and actually and really does know himself as self-knowledge.

The only way to self-knowledge is by thinking. Thinking is the steady holding of the Conscious Light within on the subject of the thinking. There are four stages or actions on the way or process of thinking. The first action is to turn the Conscious Light on the selected subject of the thinking; the second action is to hold the Conscious Light on the subject of the thinking and not to allow the thinking to be distracted by any of the myriad things that flock into the Light; the third action is the focussing of the Light on the subject; the fourth action is the focus of the Light *as a point* on the subject. Then the point of Light opens the subject into the fullness of knowledge of the subject.

These processes as actions are here stated to show the right way of thinking. They should be seen as logical and progressive thinking. But while thinking on the subject of self-knowledge, all thinking other than on that subject must be disregarded for the focus of all the Light on that subject, else there will be no actual focus of Light resulting as the real knowledge of the subject.

Three minds or ways of thinking are used by the Doer and are employed in all thinking. The purpose of the body-mind is to make contact with nature by thinking with and through the four senses, to receive impressions from nature, and to bring about whatever changes there are to be in the world. The feeling-mind is the intermediary between the body-mind and the desire-mind, to interpret and translate the impressions of nature from the body-mind to the desire-mind, and in turn to transmit the responses of the desire-mind to the impressions received.

From the early days of your childhood, you, as feeling--desire, the conscious self in the body, have allowed your body-mind to hypnotize you, so that you are in a waking self-hypnotic trance or sleep, and you are now completely under the hypnotic influence of your body-mind and the senses. Therefore you do not distinguish yourself as feeling-desire from the body you are in.

This control by the body-mind over feeling-desire makes the conscious self in every human body a slave to nature, and is the cause of the afflictions and troubles of mankind. As the conscious self, you do not distinguish yourself from the appetites and fleshly instincts and impulses, and you often do what *you* would prefer not to do, just to please your appetites and instincts. Therefore, you remain a slave to nature; you cannot escape; you do not know how to "wake up" and gain your freedom.

To wake up and be master of the body, *you* as feeling-desire must de-hypnotize yourself and learn to control your body-mind. You can do this in three steps. You take the first step by asserting yourself to yourself, and by logically reasoning to convince your body-mind of the difference and distinction between yourself and the body. The second step is to find yourself as feeling while in the body so that you can reasonably feel and understand yourself as that in the body which feels, which feels itself in the body as *not* the body. The third step is to detach, isolate, yourself and know yourself to be yourself, alone in yourself. Then you will have de-hypnotized yourself.

Confusion results when one tries to take the three steps at the same time.

In the man, desire-feeling is the conscious self in the body, because desire is the dominant representative in the male body. In the woman, feeling-desire is the conscious self in the body, because feeling is dominant in the woman body. But with man or woman, feeling must be found and freed before desire, because feeling makes the contact with nature through the four senses and holds desire to nature.

It should be an easy matter for you to prove to yourself that you are feeling-desire, distinct and distinguished from every other thing of your make-up as a human being. This you can do by understanding the difference between that of your make-up which is of nature, and that which is *you*. That of which you are only conscious through the four senses, belongs to nature; that in the make-up *as* which you are conscious, is *you*, feeling-desire—yourself.

You can begin the examination of yourself with the sense of sight, and say: "I see that person or thing;" or "This photograph is a picture of myself." But actually it cannot be *you* that sees, because you, as feeling-desire, are in the nerves and the blood, and there you cannot see or be seen. In order to see you need the sense of sight and the sense organ of sight. A person deprived of his eyes cannot see any object.

To locate yourself as in the nerves and blood and to be consciously distinct from your body—although in the body—it is necessary to understand that there are two seats of government: one of nature, and the other of yourself. Both are located in the pituitary body, a small bean-shaped organ in the brain, which is divided into a front part and a rear part.

The front part is the seat of the breath-form, which coordinates and governs the senses and the involuntary nervous system. The rear part is the seat from which you, the Doer, the conscious self, govern the voluntary system by thinking. From

93

there your body-mind reaches into the front half, acts on the breath-form there, and connects with nature by thinking through the senses.

Your body-mind thinks for nature through the senses; it does not comprehend that feeling-desire, *you*, are not of nature. It impresses you into the belief that you are the senses; that you are the body of senses. Therefore you say: "I see, hear, taste, and smell," and you continue to let your body-mind keep you hypnotized in the belief that *you* are a man body or a woman body.

There are three reasons why man has not been able to identify and distinguish himself from the physical body in which he lives. The first reason is, that he has not known what the soul or breath-form is and how it functions. The second is that he does not know that he uses three minds in thinking, that is, three ways of thinking, and what the kinds of thinking are, or what thinking is. The third reason is that he does not know that he is self-hypnotized by his body-mind. To take yourself out of the hypnosis and "wake up," you must realize that *you* are self-hypnotized. Then you can proceed with your self-de-hypnotization.

When you realize the situation and want to "wake up," you should be fully convinced that the feeling side of your conscious self is not a "fifth sense," else you cannot free yourself from the body in the present life. Feeling is not a sense at all, but is an aspect of the Doer in the human being. You can first find yourself as feeling in the body by regular and uninterrupted deep lung breathing. (*See* chapter: "REGENERATION: Breathing and the Living Soul") Then, when you detach, "isolate," your feeling from the body-mind in the breath-form, you will know and feel yourself, that is, *feel feeling as yourself*, while in the physical body, similarly as you feel the physical body as different from the garments it wears. Then you will have taken an important step forward and you will be qualified to continue your conscious progress toward full self-knowledge, that is, knowledge of the self in the body.

The pituitary body, which, as has been stated, is the seat of government for both the innumerable functions of the physical body and the activities of the Doer in the body, is the best protected part of the entire body. This is evidence of its supremely vital importance to the human make-up. It is suspended by means of a stalk, the infundibulum, from the base of the brain, like a pear by its stem, and is firmly held in place by the surrounding bony tissues. Somewhat above and behind the pituitary body, projecting slightly from the roof of the third ventricle, is the pineal body, the size of a pea. From its position in the roof of the third ventricle, the pineal body directs the Conscious Light through the infundibulum to the Doer in the rear half of the pituitary body. In the present state of things, it is largely a rudimentary organ, but it is the potential seat of the Thinker-Knower, when all three parts of the Triune Self will be in the regenerated perfect physical body.

Of great importance are the ventricles of the brain, about whose purpose anatomists have not ventured even to speculate. The ventricles are large, hollow spaces which communicate with each other. They take up a large part of the middle, and of the right and left hemispheres, of the brain. They are somewhat like a bird in configuration, the third ventricle making up the body, with the head dipping down through the infundibulum into the rear half of the pituitary body, the seat of the conscious self. The two lateral ventricles would represent the wings, and the fourth and fifth ventricles the tail which, thinning out into a threadlike canal, passes in the center of the spinal cord all the way down to the small of the back.

The Conscious Light comes from the Knower-Thinker of one's Triune Self through the top of the skull and fills the arachnoidal space between the two delicate membranes nearest to and surrounding the substances of the brain and spinal cord, as well as the ventricles in the interior of the brain. This space contains a meshwork of fine filaments and interlacing, sponge-like material between the two bounding membranes, numerous branches of arteries and veins, and a clear fluid, and communicates freely through certain well-defined apertures with the ventricles in the interior of the brain. The material in the arachnoidal space serves as conductor of the Conscious Light to the organs in the brain, by means of which the Light is made available as needed by the Doer in its thinking.

Under the guidance of the Thinker of one's Triune Self, as much Conscious Light is allotted to feeling-desire, the Doer part in the body, as that one may have. Light then goes into nature by the thinking of one's body-mind and endows it with the intelligence which is everywhere manifest in nature; and the body-mind controls but depends upon feeling-desire, without which the body-mind could not think.

It is because the body-mind controls feeling-desire in the human, that it thinks as it does. But when feeling-desire eventually de-hypnotizes itself, it will control the body-mind while it intelligently guides the thinking.

The body-mind contacting the breath-form in the front part of the pituitary body and thinking through the four senses, determines one's actions through the day; and what is thought and done during the day affects what one dreams at night. In the dream states the sense of sight is usually the active sense, and the eyes are the organs dividing the waking from the dreaming.

When the body is tired or exhausted, nature urges relaxation through the involuntary nervous system by sleep. The eyelids close, the eyeballs turn upward and inward toward a point or line; the waking state is left, and the Doer either enters the dream state or passes into dreamless sleep. In dream, the body-mind controls the Doer, and the Doer can sense and feel and desire, but in dreamless sleep the body-mind has no such control. In dreamless sleep, feeling-desire is in its own state, unconscious of the senses, and it is not in hypnosis because feeling-desire, the Doer, is then not dominated by its body-mind.

Although the body-mind is used by feeling-desire, its sphere of action is limited to the front part of the pituitary body, and as long as it contacts the front part, the Doer is still in the dream state. The rear part of the pituitary body is the domain of feeling-desire. When the body-mind connects again with the breath-form in the front part, the territory of the senses and nature, feeling-and-desire is again controlled by the body-mind.

When the Doer realizes that it is not the body and the senses, it can begin to assert itself and exercise control over the body-mind. One way to control the senses and appetites generally is by not yielding to their urges. But the particular way to control the body-mind is by suppressing its functions of thinking through sight, hearing, taste, and smell. This is done best by suppressing the function of sight during the attempts to gain the desired control. That is done by closing the eyelids and by refusing to think of any object or thing, by willing positively not to see any thing. This can be practiced at any time, but it is easier at the time for sleep. Thus one may put oneself to sleep at night as soon as he can stop thinking, and one can thereby overcome a tendency to insomnia. It is not easily done, but it can be done by persistence in the practice. When one can do it at will, he has taken a definite step toward self-mastery, and then self-de-hypnotization can be achieved.

De-hypnotization can be accomplished, not by theorizing or the belief that it may be done, but by your actually trying to *feel yourself as feeling* in the body at any time during the day. As, for example, when using the hands for any purpose, by feeling your feeling-self in the hands, and feeling the object which the hands touch; or, feeling one's leg or feet, or feeling another person in your heart. That should not be too difficult.

Distinguishing yourself at all times as different from your body makes it possible and eventually practicable for you to suppress the body-mind at will and thereby to stop its functioning. When, by thinking, you intentionally stop the functioning of the body-mind, that is to say, when you do not see, hear, taste, or smell, and remain conscious, you have suppressed the body-mind. The world has vanished, and you are alone and conscious of your feeling-self as conscious bliss!

By refusing to think on retiring, you intentionally stop thinking through the senses, and you will then be in deep sleep. Then the body-mind is detached from the breath-form in the front part and is withdrawn by feeling in the rear part of the pituitary body, and you, as feeling, are isolated from nature and alone in yourself, in deep sleep. That is automatically done for you every night when you are in dreamless sleep.

When you understand the method of procedure and do it intentionally, you subdue your body-mind to unquestioning obedience. Then, by detaching and withdrawing your body-mind from nature, you retire and know yourself *as feeling*, alone, as conscious bliss. You are in The Eternal, where time cannot be. You know yourself and are de-hypnotized. Then, in your safe abode, your body-mind goes into the breath-form and contacts nature by thinking through the senses. You are again in the world, but you are not deluded; you perceive things as they really are, and the body-mind does not attempt to rule; it serves. Then you know and feel yourself to be as distinct and different from the body. You can, when in union with your desire, complete the victory.

REGENERATION: The Parts Played by Breathing and the Breath-Form or "Living Soul"

The great endeavor to find and be on The Great Way includes the regeneration of the human physical body and its restoration to The Realm of Permanence in which the Doer of each Triune Self once was, and which it left because of the "original sin," so-called, as explained in later pages.

Ever since that dim and distant past, each Doer has walked the face of the earth, in one human body after another, driven and impelled by unknown forces toward an unseen task—which is, to return to its former home, The Realm of Permanence, or Garden of Eden, or Paradise. This return to its home involves, of necessity, the regeneration of the human body into a perfect, sexless, immortal physical body, not subject to the ordinary needs of physical existence.

The structure of the human body is of solid food, water, and air; and the life of the body is in the blood. But the life of the blood and builder of the body is the breath-form, and the kind of body built is determined by the thinking.

The breath-form of the human is the intermediary between nature and the Doer of the Triune Self. It is a unit, an unintelligent unit of nature, which nevertheless is indissolubly connected with the Doer to which it belongs. It has an active and a passive side. The active side is the breath of the breath-form and the passive side is the form or "the soul." The form of the breath-form is present at the time of copulation and is in the mother during pregnancy, but the breath of the breath-form, although inseparable from the form, is not in the mother during pregnancy; its presence there would interfere with the mother's breath, which is that which builds up the body of the fetus. At the moment of birth, with the first gasp, the breath part of the breath-form enters the infant and connects with it through the heart and lungs. And thereafter, the breath-form never ceases to breathe until death; on the leaving of the breath-form the body dies.

The form of the breath-form is the pattern on which the food that is taken in is built into the body. The breath through breathing is the builder of the physical body. That is the secret of tissue building: breathing builds the cells. It builds them up by anabolism, as it is called, and eliminates the waste-matter by catabolism, so-called, and it balances the building and elimination by metabolism.

Now the breath-form has on it as a basic design, when it comes into the world, the sexlessness of the perfect body from which it originally came. If that were not so, one could never regenerate the body to its original condition of perfection as of sexlessness from The Realm of Permanence. So, automatically, under observation of one's own Triune Self, the body develops from infancy to childhood; and childhood is distinguished from infancy by the coming of feeling-desire, the Doer, into the body. The evidence of this is that previously the child did not ask questions, but is simply trained to repeat as a parrot does.

When the Doer has come into the body and begins to ask questions, its thinking makes impressions on the breath-form. Its form is the memory-tablet on which all impressions from nature or of whatever kind are impressed, and it holds the impressions. Those are the memory-tablets.

The human memory is limited to the impressions of the four senses, so that all our memory is limited to those four senses; and the thing that impresses it is the recognition or attention that is given by the Doer to these subjects.

The breathing comes in and goes out from the beginning to the end of life. There is a definite life-span for the individual, the Doer, which it has made in the past. It has made that span of life by its thinking, and if it keeps on the line of this thinking it will die as it has ordained.

But if it changes its thinking from death to immortal life, there is a possibility of transforming its body from a body of sexuality and death to a perfect, sexless and immortal physical body, to return to The Realm of Permanence from which it originally fell. The accomplishment depends on being able to see things as those things really are, and to determine to do what one believes is right and possible for one to do; and it depends on the will to carry out its determination into accomplishment.

When one determines on that accomplishment, consequences of past actions might arise to lead away from success. The ordinary affairs in the life of one who so determines will furnish all the trials and temptations and allurements: the glamour of the senses, the appetites, and emotions to distract it. And chief among them is sexuality, in any form. These attractions and impulses and instincts are the real and actual facts of the initiations and tests and trials of all allegorical statements that are made concerning the "mysteries" and "initiations." One's ordinary experiences in life give all the means for one's deciding what to do and what not to do, in order to reach one's goal. The different ages through which the child passes all have a part in the ultimate result. The adolescent period is the turning-point as to what it will at first do; and that is the point at which the sex of its body asserts itself, when the germ cells of the male and the female are determined, and which prompt the thinking of the Doer of the body in which it is.

One begins to think of one's sex in relation to the other sex. And the thinking concerning these basic facts of human life cause the breath-form to perform the important biological changes in the germ cell.

The germ cell as sperm in the male must divide itself twice. The first division is to throw off the sexlessness of the germ cell. It is now a female-male or hermaphrodite cell. The second division is to throw off the femaleness. Then it is a male cell, and competent to impregnate. In the female body, the first division of the ovum is to throw off the sexlessness. Then the ovum is a male-female cell. The second division is to throw off the maleness. Then it is a female cell ready to be impregnated.

Now this is the ordinary human sexual condition. If the thought in the beginning had not been impelled by the sexual body in which it was, there would have been no divisions of the sex germ in a male or female body, and the thinking would have built the body into a regenerated body according to the original, basic plan on the form of the breath-form.

Because the form of the breath-form is basically sexless, it carries its original form of sexlessness on it, from when it left The Realm of Permanence, and that can never be erased. And however long it takes, through any number of lives, the Doer of the Triune Self must and will determine to regenerate its body, and the Doer must do this in some one life.

This is determined by the Doer's experiences, the learning from the experiences, and the knowledge that is acquired from the learning; and this leads the Doer in some life to make the effort toward the accomplishment. And the accomplishment must be in one body, because conscious immortality cannot be achieved after death. That is so because there is no body after death which it can make immortal. The Doer must have a physical body to make that body immortal.

The body to be made immortal is not a non-physical body. It has to be a solid, fleshly physical body, because the physical

102

body possesses all the material necessary for it to change and transform the ordinary physical sexual mortal body into a perfect and immortal physical body, on which the changes of time can have no effect.

Those who merely care about maintaining the physical world according to the order of sexual bodies are not interested in taking the right way. They are interested in maintaining human things as they are—that is, according to sexuality and death. But in order to attain immortality, death must be conquered, because every human body wears, and is, a costume of death.

Death has its hand on every body that comes into this world, and with every body, death prevails in the changes that go on. The fairest face of man or maid is but a mask of death. And immortality is gained by the conquering of death; and death is based on the sexes.

Therefore, the changes which must go on in the male or female body must be made in one continuous body until the body is changed from the physical structure of death—male or female—by regeneration and transformation into a sexless body, by which death is conquered with the conquering of sexuality. Therefore, conscious immortality cannot be achieved after the body dies.

After death, the conscious self, having left the body, can think over only what it has thought during the life on earth. No new thinking is done after death. Its breath-form is with it; but it cannot change its breath-form after death. Thinking must write its prescriptions on the form of the breath-form in a living human body. No biological changes can go on after death; and the biological processes are carried on according to order by the thinking of the Doer on its breath-form. The biological processes work according to that thinking.

All human beings occupy bodies composed of sex cells because of the prevailing acceptance of the marriage relationship. It is that upon which our society is based. Indeed, all nature exists through sex, and because of sex. Sex ties humans to nature. And the means of passing from this world of sex and death and rebirth is through the abnegation of sex completely in thought and deed, thereby rebuilding the body according to its original pattern composed of sexless cells by preventing the divisions in the making of the sperm and ovum. And since this cannot be done after death, it must be achieved while there is life in the body. The body is the means, too, of our getting back to The Realm of Permanence. The appetites through the senses chain us to nature, and only by breaking these chains through intelligent reasoning do we destroy the attachments. Unattached, one is free. And freedom is the state in which one lives who is unattached.

No thought of sexuality must be entertained in the heart or in the brain of one who self-determines his immortality in one life. And the thinking in any one life will contribute to bring about the conditions for the accomplishment of the object of one's thinking. When the thinking is for immortality, the conditions will be furnished. The people, the places, the situations, though he knows it not, will be determined by one's thinking. They will all converge to the life in which he determines to become consciously immortal in a physical body, even to his present life. His Thinker and Knower see to it. Nothing is done by chance; everything is done by law and order. There is no chance. We do not have to look after our Thinker and Knower to see that they do their part. The only thing with which one is concerned is the performance of his own duties. And one determines his duties by his attitude in thinking.

One's own Thinker and Knower will protect the Doer to the extent and the degree that the Doer will allow itself to be protected. Because, although there is no communication between the Doer in the body and its Thinker-Knower, which is not in the body, there *is* a means of communication through rightness and reason, which is the voice of rightness as the law and of reason as the justice.

Rightness as the law says, "no, do not," when the Doer would go against what is right and what it should not do. And as to what it *should* do, it can consult itself within. And what seems reasonable and proper for it to do, that it should do. In this way there can be communication for one who desires communication between the Doer in the body and its Thinker-Knower.

The difference is, the body-mind tells the Doer what it should do according to the senses. And this, expediency, is the law of the human world: what the senses suggest. It may be right and proper concerning strictly physical matters. But concerning the path of immortality, in which the Doer is interested, expediency must be subject to the law of rightness and justice from within.

Therefore, for one to know what he should do, or what he should not do, he should consult himself from within, and do what he does because of his confidence that nothing will go wrong, actually, if he does what he knows is right for *him* to do. That is the law for one who desires immortality.

In the course of time, wonderful and miraculous changes will be brought about in his body without his knowing what is being done. But these changes toward immortality are carried on mostly by the involuntary nervous system. He need pay no attention to these changes, although he will be conscious of them in due time. But the changes can be made only by what he thinks, and by what he does—that is, structural changes.

Concerning the actual changes, he needs only know the simplest and most direct way of causing the changes. This is by intentional, regular, complete and deep lung breathing—in-breathing and out-breathing. There are four different kinds of breathing: physical breathing, form-breathing, life-breathing, and light-breathing; and each of these four breathings has four subdivisions. He need not be concerned about the subdivisions and the kinds of breathing, because he will be made aware of them in the course of his breathing, if he continues on the course.

But he should understand about the different kinds intellectually. No human breathes properly, completely, because he does not fill his lungs with the little air that he breathes. Filling his lungs with each in-breathing allows time for all the blood that passes through to be oxygenated, and for the blood cells to carry the oxygen to the cellular structure in the physical body.

Few humans breathe more than one tenth of the amount that they should take in with each in-breathing. Therefore their cells die and have to be rebuilt; they are partly starved. Then with each proper out-breathing there are expelled from the venous blood accumulated impurities before the next regular in-breathing. A definite time each day should be given to proper in-breathing and out-breathing—as long a period as one can give at any time of the day or night—perhaps half an hour each in the morning and in the evening.

This regular uninterrupted breathing should be carried on at set intervals until it becomes habitual throughout the day. When the cells throughout the body are being supplied with the necessary oxygen, the subdivisions of the physical body will be supplied with their subsidiary breaths (the molecules in the cells, the atoms in the molecules, and the electrons and other particles in the atoms). And when that is done, one's body will be immune to disease: he cannot be infected.

This may take many years or many lives. But one who wants to learn how to live should try to "live in The Eternal." Then the time element will not worry him so much. In the meantime, when he understands the regular physical breathing, he begins to pay attention to where the breath goes in the body. This he does by feeling and thinking. If he feels where the breath is going throughout the body, he must think about it. As he thinks, he feels where the breath is going. He should not try to carry the breath into any particular part. All he needs to do is feel where it *does* go.

The breath must go to all parts of the body for the body to keep alive and in proper condition. And the fact that one does not ordinarily feel where the breath goes in the body, does not prevent it from going throughout the body. But if his thinking and feeling is to feel where the breath does go, this will charge the blood and open the spaces in the body, so that all parts of the body will come to life and be kept alive. And it is also a means of his knowing something about the structure of the body.

When one is not in real health the fact is evidenced by his not feeling all parts of the body when attempting to do so; that is, wherever the blood and nerves go. And since the blood and nerves are the fields, respectively, in which desire and feeling operate, one should be conscious wherever the blood and the nerves are, which is throughout the entire body. As one rejuvenates the body by breathing and can feel the blood and nerves *in* the body, he will learn whatever he *should* learn about the body in his breathing, which may be at any time. But when he has his body in perfect health, it will mean that he has completed his course of the physical breathing. He does not have to bother to try to find out, because the processes will make themselves known to him, and he will become conscious of the changes in the course of his thinking and breathing.

As he goes on there will come a time when the form of the breath-form will begin to change. This is done not by his decision; it is automatically adjusted in the course of his thinking. This course will lead to the form-breathing after the physical breathing has prepared the physical ground. Then, when the form-breathing begins, an inner body begins to form, and that inner body will be a sexless form. Why? Because his thinking has *not* been according to thoughts of sex, which used to cause the biological change in the germ cells. And, the form of the breath-form having a clear form of sexlessness, the body will begin to be built in its structure according to the pattern of the breath-form, which is sexlessness.

At this period, the practitioner of this process needs no further instruction from exterior sources, because he will be able to communicate with his Thinker-Knower, who will be his guide.

REGENERATION: By Right Thinking

The manner in which the thinking of the body-mind on subjects and objects of the senses attaches Conscious Light to the things thought of has been described in the chapter, "KNOW THYSELF, and The Finding of the Conscious Self in the Body." The Light going into nature by this means directs the units of nature in building up the structure of the human body; and Light thus sent out by thinking bears the stamp of the one who thinks. The knowledge acquired by thinking through the senses is sense-knowledge, which changes as the senses change. Sense-knowledge is acquired by the Doer, feeling-desire, thinking in accordance with the body-mind through the senses; it is always changing because nature is always changing.

But when the body-mind is subdued by the thinking of the minds of feeling-desire, then the Doer will control the body-mind and will see and understand nature because the Conscious Light shows all things as they really are. Feeling-desire will then know that all matter should be in The Eternal Order of Progression instead of being retarded in rounds of circulation by human beings in this human world of change.

It is essential to understand that the front part of the pituitary body in the middle of the brain is the central station from which the breath-form coordinates the four senses with the involuntary nervous system for nature; that the rear part of the pituitary body is the central station from where the conscious self as feeling-desire thinks and acts through the voluntary nervous system; that the body-mind thinks only through the four senses; that Conscious Light in thinking is given by the Doer to its body-mind and sent into nature, and is thus attached to the objects of nature; and, therefore, that feeling-desire does not distinguish itself as beyond nature, as not of nature.

By thinking, feeling-desire binds persons, places, and things to itself and binds itself to them and, being bound, is enslaved. To be free, it must free itself. It can free itself by detaching itself from the things to which it is bound, and, by remaining unattached, it is free.

The Light which shows the way to freedom and immortal life is the Conscious Light within. As it enters the brain, it extends by way of the spinal cord and nerves to all parts of the body. The spinal cord with its numerous branches is the tree of life in the body. When one wholeheartedly desires freedom from sexuality, the Light illuminates the darkness of the body and, in the course of events, the body is changed and transformed from darkness to light. The light of the senses is of time, of the changes of time, as measured by day and night, by life and death. The Conscious Light is of The Eternal, where time cannot be. The Conscious Light is in and through this man-and-woman-world of birth and death, but the way out of the darkness cannot be seen through the eyes of flesh and blood. One must see the way through the eyes of understanding until the way through the darkness is clearly seen. The fear of time or darkness or death vanishes as Light on the way becomes strong and steadfast. One who is convinced of the way to deathlessness will so think and act that the thinking and the acting continue uninterruptedly. If the Doer in the body is not ready to transform it in the present life, it will pass through death and awaken in the next life to continue in the new body the transformation of the human into a sexless body of perfection.

The outer form and structure of the body are known in detail. The paths of the nerves have been explored, and the relations between the motor nerves of the conscious self and the sensory nerves of nature are known. In addition to what has been said about the seat of the nature government being in the front part of the pituitary body and that of the Doer government being in the rear part, it is here stated that during waking hours the division between the rear part and the front part of the pituitary body is bridged by the body-mind which reaches over from the rear part to the fore part to think for nature through the senses. It has been known that there is a switchboard called the red center (red nucleus) which at all times automatically connects and relates the motor nerves with the sensory nerves determining all actions of the body. This red center or switchboard, one each to the right and to the left of the median line, is located under or behind the pineal body near the four little bulges, called the quadrigemina, in the third ventricle. All these parts and nerves are concerned with the physical corporeal functions of the brain. But no explanation has heretofore been given of the functioning of the conscious self in the body, without which the human body would be an animal devoid of power to determine the actions, or to understand the structure or functioning of the body.

Feeling-desire in the body is not corporeal, nor is it of the senses. It cannot be found by scalpel or microscope. But the conscious self can be found and known by persistent systematic breathing and feeling and thinking, especially as described in the preceding chapter.

For one who desires to know the conscious self in the body, it is necessary to have some definite understanding of the meanings and the distinctions between the terms "matter" and "mind," and to understand that there are three minds or ways of thinking, which the Doer uses: the body-mind, feeling-mind, and desire-mind. The dictionaries are not of much help in this respect.

Webster defines "matter" as "That of which any physical object is composed." But this definition is inadequate to supply the all-inclusiveness and requirements of the term; and he defines "mind" as "Memory; specifically: a state of remembering—," but his definition of mind does not at all deal with the meaning or operation of the word.

It is therefore well to consider the meaning of the terms "matter" and "mind" as they are used in this book. All matter of whatever kind is of units in orderly and sequential stages of development. But there is a sharp and distinct difference between nature units and intelligent units in degree of their being conscious. Nature units are conscious *as* their functions *only*; and all nature units are unintelligent. An intelligent unit is a Triune Self unit that has passed beyond nature. It is composed of three inseparable parts: the I-ness and selfness as the Knower or noetic part; the rightness and reason as the Thinker or mental part; and the feeling and desire as the Doer or psychic part. Only one portion of the Doer part of feeling-desire is embodied in a human at any one time; and that one portion is the representative of all its other portions. The terms used in speaking of a Triune Self as a unit composed of so many and various parts and portions are awkward and inadequate, but there are no other terms in the language which will allow an exact description or explanation.

The definitions quoted above are misunderstandings of what memory is, and of what mind is or does. Briefly, memory is the record made on the breath-form by the impressions of sight, hearing, taste, or smell, like the impressions made on film in photography. Memory is the reproduction or copy of the picture. The eye is the camera through which the picture is seen by perceptiveness through the sense of sight and impressed on the breath-form as the film. The reproduction is the counterpart or the remembering of the record. All the instruments used in seeing and in remembering are of nature.

The term "mind" as used here is that function or process with which or by which thinking is done. Mind is the functioning of the intelligent matter of the conscious self, as distinguished from the functioning of the unintelligent matter of the four senses by the body-mind. The conscious self cannot think of itself or identify itself as apart from the body because, as stated before, it is under hypnotic control of its body-mind and is therefore compelled by the body-mind to think in terms of the senses. And the body-mind cannot think of feeling-desire as not of the senses.

To distinguish itself, the conscious self must have control over its body-mind, because such control is necessary in order to think in terms of the Triune Self, instead of thinking in terms of objects of the senses. It is through this control that the thinking of the body-mind will, in the course of time, regenerate and transform the human sexual body into a perfect sexless physical body, by vitalizing and changing the blood of the human body through breathing of the life eternal, when the body is made ready to receive eternal life as told in the preceding chapter. Then feeling-desire has understanding of itself.

When feeling-and-desire are inseparably one Doer part of the Triune Self, they will be beauty and power in right relation with the Thinker and Knower, as a Knower-Thinker-Doer Triune Self complete, and will take its place in The Realm of Permanence.

As one or more human beings understand and begin to bring about these transformations in themselves, other humans will surely follow. Then this world of birth and death will gradually change from the delusions and illusions of the body-mind and senses by becoming more and more conscious of the Realities within and beyond. The conscious Doers in their bodies will then understand and perceive The Realm of Permanence as they conceive and understand themselves in the changing bodies in which they are.

The Perfect Sexless
Immortal Physical Body

What does the immortal physical body of a Triune Self look like?

Such a body in The Realm of Permanence is the ever-present and complete embodiment of permanent knowledge and conscious power in transcendent beauty. In looking at a perfect sexless physical body, no sexual thought would be supposed or considered by man or by woman. But no human being could see a Triune Self as it is in The Realm of Permanence. Were a Triune Self to appear to a mortal in the human world, its appearance would be what that Triune Self knew that it should be: appropriate to the occasion, and not otherwise.

The body of a Triune Self is the personalized physical expression of the Identity and Knowledge, the Rightness and Reason, and the Beauty and Power of that Triune Self.

In this human physical world anyone may stand in the sunlight and feel its warmth; but no sensible person would try to look at the face of the sun in order to paint its features and show the light as it shines upon and illumines the earth.

To get an idea of the appearance of the body of a complete Triune Self in The Realm of Permanence, or "Kingdom of God," one should understand that only one portion of the Doer part of its Triune Self is in the male or female body; whereas the perfect physical body of the Triune Self has all of twelve portions of the Doer perfectly related and balanced in inseparable union and, therefore, is neither male nor female. The perfections of all the twelve portions are composed in the balanced expression of beauty and power.

But let it be supposed that a man or a woman could and were to look on such a perfect body! What then? Then the man would think of it as a being so divinely beautiful and of such superior excellence as to be loved in reverence and to be contemplated as the Godhead. And a woman would look upon it as a being so great and so supremely powerful as to be loved in worshipful adoration and by the giving of herself in service and obedience to its least request or command. For a mortal to look on a perfect physical body in The Realm of Permanence would evoke love in both man and woman. To be in such a body would mean the blending and amalgamation of desire-feeling and feeling-desire into, or as, one being of supernal beauty and conscious power. Then its body is the perfect physical expression of the conscious self. Men and women must understand that if they would know what the perfect physical body of a Triune Self looks like in The Realm of Permanence, they must comprehend how omniscience and omnipotence and omnipresence are expressed in a sexless physical body. That is what the immortal physical body of a Triune Self looks like in perfect poise.

In looking at such a body, each human being would see expressed its own inherent hope, its longings, its yearnings, its true and pent-up deep-seated heart's desire, fully and completely expressed in that perfect body—as the pattern or model it itself is to be when it has performed its duty to itself, to its Thinker and Knower, and to nature.

The human body is built up and composed of cells: unbalanced cells which are arranged and maintained according to four systems—the digestive, circulatory, respiratory, and generative systems. The food or structure of the body is of the unbalanced units of earth, water, air and light, which are in continuous circulations of the human world. The circulations are kept up by the breath in its breathing. By its breathing in

115

and breathing out, the breath is the maintenance of the unbalanced cells, the life and the death of the body. The first intake of the breath at birth, and the last outgo at death, mark the beginning and the end of the corporeal human body.

Birth makes sexual intercourse necessary, and birth is the penalty for the male and female bodies of unbalanced cells. Death of the body is the penalty of the incorporeal conscious self for not balancing its feeling-desire and restoring itself and its body to consciously immortal life in The Realm of Permanence.

When the Doer returns to The Realm of Permanence in its then perfect and immortal body, the Doer will be in conscious at-one-ment with its Thinker and Knower. Then the Doer will have achieved victory over death. The immortal body will not need the gross, unbalanced foods of the human world. The immortal body will breathe the balanced units of The Eternal Order of Progression. The body will then have been regenerated and reconstituted to its original form, having four "brains"—the cranial, thoracic, abdominal, and pelvic brains. Then it will breathe the balanced, transient units, conscious only as their functions as laws of nature through the worlds, as explained in the book *Thinking and Destiny*.

The perfect body here spoken of is complete. Nothing can be added to it; nothing can be taken from it; it cannot be improved; it is a body sufficient in itself.

The original form of that perfect body is graven on the breath-form of each human being, and the preparation for its rebuilding will begin when the human being stops thinking of or letting the thought of sex enter, or in any way stimulate the desire for sex which leads to the act of sex. This is so, because such thinking causes the breath-form to change the germ cells of the body to become male or female sex cells. The age of the body has little to do with the matter. So long as the human will continue the practice of uninterrupted deep lung breathing, and feel where the breath goes, and think to understand where the feeling with the breathing goes, that one can reconstitute and transform the male or female body into a perfect sexless and immortal physical body.

As one or more human beings understand and begin to bring about these transformations in themselves, other human beings will surely follow. Then this world of birth and death will gradually change from the delusions and illusions produced by the body-mind and the senses. Human beings will become more and more conscious of the Realities within and beyond. The conscious Doers in their bodies will then understand and perceive The Realm of Permanence as they conceive and understand themselves in the changing bodies in which they are.

Slavery or Freedom?

W ebster says that slavery is: "The condition of a slave; bondage. Continued and wearisome labor, drudgery." And also that a slave is: "A person held in bondage. One who has lost control of himself, as to vice, lust, etc."

Stated plainly, human slavery is the state or condition in which a person is obliged to live in bondage to a master and to nature, who must obey the demands of master and of nature, without regard to his choice as to what he would or would not do.

The word freedom, as used in this book, is the state or condition of the self of desire-and-feeling as the conscious Doer in the body when it has detached itself from nature and remains unattached. Freedom is: To be and will and do and have, without attachment to any object or thing of the four senses. That means that one is not attached in thought to any object or thing of nature, and that one will not attach oneself to anything. Attachment means bondage. Intentional detachment means freedom from bondage.

Human slavery is specifically concerned with the conscious self in the body. The conscious self is urged and goaded even against its will to yield to the appetites, lusts and passions engendered by the nature of the body in which it is bound. Instead of being the master of the body, the self may become the slave of alcohol, drugs, or tobacco, as it always is the slave of sex.

This slavery is of the conscious self in the body of the "free man," as well as in the body of the bond slave to his owner. So it must continue until the self knows that it is not the body in which it is enslaved; whereas, by finding and freeing oneself from slavery to the body, one would thereby immortalize the body and be greater than the learned men and rulers of the world.

In ancient times, when the ruler of a people desired to conquer another ruler, he would lead his forces to battle into that other's territory. And, if successful, he could drag the conquered ruler at the wheels of his chariot if he so willed.

History tells us that Alexander the Great is the most remarkable example of a world conqueror. Born in 356 B.C., he gained power over all Greece; conquered Tyre and Gaza; was crowned on the throne of Egypt, as Pharaoh; founded Alexandria; destroyed the Persian power; defeated Porus in India; and then withdrew from India to Persia. As death was near he asked Roxane, his favorite wife, to secretly drown him in the Euphrates River so that people would believe, from his disappearance, that he was a God, as he had claimed, and had returned to the race of Gods. Roxane refused. He died in Babylon, a world conqueror at the age of 33. Just before his death, on being asked to whom he would leave his conquests, he was able to answer only in a whisper: "To the strongest." He died in slavery to his ambitions—a bond slave to his appetites and outrageous feelings and desires. Alexander conquered kingdoms of the earth, but he was himself conquered by his own baseness.

But, with Alexander as a conspicuous example, why and how is man made a slave to nature by his own feelings and desires? To understand that, it is necessary to see where feeling-and-desire is in the physical body, and how, by its own doing, it is controlled and enslaved by nature. This will be seen from the relation of the physical body to its feeling-and-desire self within the body.

119

This relation—to briefly recapitulate—is carried on for nature by means of the involuntary nervous system, and for the conscious self by the voluntary nervous system, as follows: The senses are the roots of nature in the breath-form, in the front part of the pituitary body. Feeling-and-desire—as the conscious self, with the body-mind, feeling-mind and desire-mind—is located in the rear part. These two parts of the pituitary are thus adjoining central stations for nature and for the conscious self. The body-mind cannot think of or for feeling-and-desire. It must, therefore, so to say, reach over from the rear part to the front part of the pituitary to think through the senses for nature in the breath-form; and to think it must have the Conscious Light.

The *feelings* of feeling, as sensations, are carried into nature. The forms of nature are the typal forms as animal and plant forms in nature. They are furnished by the Doer after death, when it temporarily puts off its sensual desire forms; it takes them on again during the next fetal development, and deals with them after entering the new human body during the youth and growth of the body. The thoughts of the human during life maintain the forms of nature by thinking.

The words feeling and desire, slave, slavery, and freedom, are here given more distinct and specific definitions and meanings than in dictionaries. Here, feeling-and-desire is shown to be oneself. *You are* feeling-and-desire. When you, as feeling-and-desire, quit the body, the body is dead, but *you* will go on through the after-death states, and will return to earth to take on another human body that will have been prepared for *you*, the conscious incorporeal feeling-desire self. But while you are in the physical body you are not free; you are a slave to the body. You are bound to nature by the senses and appetites and cravings stronger than chains ever bound the bond slave as a chattel slave to the master he served. The chattel slave knew he was a slave. But you are more or less a willing slave without knowing that you are a slave.

Therefore you are in a situation worse than was the bond slave. Whereas he knew that he was not the master, you do not distinguish yourself from the physical body through which you are enslaved. On the other hand, you are in a situation better than the bond slave, because he could not free himself from the slavery to his master. But there is hope for you, because, if you will, you can distinguish yourself from the body and its senses, by thinking. By thinking you can understand that you do think, and that the body does not and cannot think. That is the first point. Then you can understand that the body cannot do anything without you, and it compels you to obey its demands as dictated by the senses in all occupations; and further, that you are so occupied and impressed with the thinking about sensuous objects and subjects that you do not distinguish yourself as feeling-desire, and as being different from the sensations of the feelings and desires of or for the senses.

Feelings and desires are not sensations. Sensations are not feelings and desires. What is the difference? Feelings and desires are extensions from feeling-desire in the kidneys and adrenals to the nerves and blood where they meet the impact of the units of nature coming through the senses. Where the units contact the feelings and desires in the nerves and blood, the units are the sensations.

Human slavery has been an institution from immemorial time. That is to say, human beings have owned as their own property the bodies and lives of other human beings—by capture, war, purchase or hereditary rights—in all stages of society, from aboriginal barbarism to cultures of civilizations. The buying and selling of slaves was carried on as a matter of course, without question or dispute. Not until the 17th century did a few people, called abolitionists, publicly begin to condemn slavery. Then the number of abolitionists increased and so did their activities and condemnation of slavery and the slave trade. In 1787 the abolitionists in England found a real and inspired leader in William Wilberforce. During 20 years he fought for the suppression of the slave trade, and after that for the freedom of the slaves. In 1833 the Emancipation Act was carried. The British Parliament thereby put an end to slavery throughout the British Empire. Thirty-two years later, in the United States, The Emancipation Act for freeing the slaves was proclaimed during the Civil War and became an actual fact in 1865.

But freedom from ownership and slavery of bodies is only the beginning of real human freedom. Now we have to face the astonishing fact that the conscious individuals in the human bodies are slaves to their bodies. The conscious individual is incorporeal, intelligent, beyond nature. Nevertheless, he is a slave. In fact, he is so devoted a slave to the body that he identifies himself with and as the body.

The conscious self in the body speaks of itself as the name of its body, and one is known and identified by that name. From the time the body is old enough to be taken care of, one works for it, feeds it, cleanses it, clothes it, exercises it, trains and adorns it, worships it in devotional service throughout its life; and when at the end of its days the self leaves the body, the name of that body is graven on a headstone or tomb erected on the grave. But the unknown conscious self, *you*, would thereafter be spoken of as the body in the grave.

We, the conscious selves, have re-existed in bodies throughout the ages, and have dreamed of ourselves as the bodies in which we then dreamt. It is time to become conscious that we are slaves to the bodies in which we dream, awake or asleep. As the slaves were conscious as slaves who desired freedom, so must we, the conscious slaves in physical bodies, be conscious of our slavery and desire freedom, emancipation, from our bodies which are our masters.

This is the time to think and work for our real emancipation—for the individual freedom of our conscious selves from the bodies in which we live, so that by our becoming conscious as Doer selves we will have changed and transformed our bodies to be superhuman bodies.

It is high time for each conscious self to truly understand that life after life through the ages we have been desire-feeling in a male body, or feeling-desire in a female body.

Let us ask ourselves: "What is life?" The answer is: You, I, We, have been and are feeling-and-desire—dreaming of ourselves through nature. Life is that, and nothing more or less than that. Now we can affirm and determine that we will diligently strive to discover and to distinguish ourselves within our bodies, and to free ourselves from slavery to our bodies.

Now is the beginning of the real Emancipation—the emancipation of the conscious self in the human body, unconscious that it is the slave of the sexual body that is its master. This age-old slavery has been going on since the days of the legendary Adam, when each conscious self now in a human body became, first, an Adam, and then an Adam and Eve. (*See* chapter, "THE STORY OF ADAM AND EVE: The Story of Every Human Being"). Marriage is the oldest institution in the world. It is so old that people say it is natural, but that does not make it right and proper. The slave-self has made itself a slave. But that happened long ago and is forgotten. Scripture is quoted to prove that it is right and proper. And it is written in the lawbooks and justified in all law courts of the land.

There are many who will recognize that this self-slavery is wrong. These will be the new abolitionists who will condemn the practice and try to abolish the self-slavery. But large numbers will in all probability ridicule the thought and offer long established evidence that there is no such thing as self-slavery; that mankind is composed of male and female bodies; that physical slavery was a fact in civilized lands; but that self-slavery is a delusion, an aberration of the mind.

However, it is to be expected that others will see and understand the facts concerning self-slavery and engage in telling about it and work for self-emancipation from our sexual bodies in which all are slaves. Then gradually and in due time the facts will be seen and the subject will be dealt with for the good of all mankind. If we do not learn to know ourselves in this civilization, it will be destroyed. So the opportunity for self-knowledge has been deferred in all past civilizations. And we, our conscious selves will have to await the coming of a future civilization to achieve self-knowledge.

Victory Over Sin and Death

Why should man and woman continue their practices of sexuality—attended by premature debility and hastening death—when they can begin a period of enlightened living, ultimately leading one to be self-consciously immortal in deathless and glorious physical bodies?

The way begins in darkness and continues through trouble and struggle and trial; but, by the Conscious Light within, the way eventually opens into and as Conscious Bliss in The Eternal.

Webster states that "Sin is the transgression of the law of God, iniquity," and that "Death is the cessation of all vital functions without capability of resuscitation."

It is said in Scripture that Adam and Eve committed the first and original sin by transgression of the first law of God, which was, that they should not have sexual union, because they would thereafter surely die; and that as desire-feeling they could not again live as a man and a woman together in one body. After that they would re-exist as desire-feeling in a male body, or as feeling-desire in a female body.

Let it be understood that every man or woman was aforetime an Adam and Eve in the Realm of Eden. And that because of their "sin" they were expelled from the interior of the earth onto its outer surface—and they died. Their bodies died because sin, as sexuality, is surely and necessarily followed by death. But, as the desire-feeling in man, or as feeling-desire in woman, they cannot die.

Each man or woman now on earth was in the beginning, as the Bible cryptically states, an Adam in the Garden of Eden. That means, as stated in this book, that the present human body was "in the beginning" a sexless body. The "Doer," the psychic part of each one's Triune Self, as feeling-desire, could not be "balanced" in the sexless Adam body because it needed a male body and a female body to serve as two scales as balances and so to have free exercise of its feeling-mind and desire-mind in thinking of each other. The body-mind therefore acted as the trial-test by its thinking of their bodies only. The body-mind could not think otherwise than of their bodies.

The putting of Adam to sleep and taking "a rib" from which Eve was made, signifies the period during which there was the separation of the sexless Adam into the male Adam body and the female Eve body. The "rib" was taken from a then front- or nature-spinal column, of which the sternum is the vestigial remains, and which in the perfect body, was called the tree of the Knowledge of Good and Evil, descending to and connecting with what is now called the pubic bone.

Of this front-spinal column, or the "tree of the Knowledge of Good and Evil," the "Lord God," according to the Bible, said: "... thou shalt not eat of it: for in the day that thou eatest thereof thou shalt surely die." (Genesis 2, v. 17)

The Bible story of Adam and Eve is a mystery, an enigma; it is cryptic, puzzling, and seems to be inscrutable. But if it is read with the above as a key, the story makes sense and loses its inscrutability. It is a mystery given to mankind which every man or woman must eventually and individually solve.

Every man and every woman is the individual lock and key to the mystery—the lock being the physical body of man or woman, and the key, the individual conscious self of desire-feeling in the man, and that of feeling-desire in the woman.

The mystery will be solved by man and by woman when the individual conscious self of desire-feeling understands and finds itself in the man body, or that of feeling-desire finds itself in the woman body; and at the same time the active-passive units of the male body and the passive-active units of the female body will be equilibrated and balanced. Thus, each conscious self is to regenerate and transform and resurrect its male or female body of sexuality and death into a perfect sexless and immortal physical body, and so to redeem and restore it to its Lord God, its Father in Heaven: that is, a complete Knower-Thinker-Doer—The Triune Self in the Realm of Permanence. That is the story from Adam to Jesus, and of the coming of "The Kingdom of God." That is the destiny for each and every human being.

Continence

The reader may ask what physiologists and physicians have to say about continence and the marriage relation with regard to the health of the body.

This very vital subject has been sadly neglected in medical literature by writers on genito-urinary and neurological subjects. An outstanding authority on diseases of men and women, Max Huhner, states in his "Disorders of the Sexual Function in the Male and Female," that he went to the trouble some years ago to consult a great many textbooks on physiology, but found "that not one of them had anything to say on the question. Other authorities, not physiologists, however, have expressed opinions on the subject, among them no less an authority than Prof. Bryant, the great English surgeon, who states that the function of the sexual glands may be suspended for a long time, possibly for life, and yet their structure may be sound and capable of being roused into activity on any healthy stimulation. Unlike other glands or tissues in general, they do not waste or atrophy prematurely for want of use. And it is pointed out that the sexual glands are constructed on entirely different principles from most of the other organs of the body. They are constructed for intermittent action and their function may be suspended indefinitely without harm to either their anatomy or physiology. Witness the mammary gland. A woman becomes pregnant and gives birth to a child, and immediately the gland, which had remained dormant for years, swells up and secretes milk. After lactation is finished, the gland becomes smaller and inactive. She may not become pregnant again for another ten or more years, and during all this time the gland is not in use, but even after this long period, should she again become pregnant, it will again swell up and be absolutely useful in spite of the long period of disuse. The author says that he has gone somewhat into detail into this question, because it is very important and is constantly being brought up by the opponents of the subject of continence and is very apt to impress the laity."

Other authorities say: "... there is yet comfort for the unmarried man in those pages which show that perfect continence is quite compatible with perfect health, and thus a great load is at once lifted from the mind of him who wishes to be conscientious as well as virile and in health with all the organs of the body performing their proper functions." And again: "It is pernicious, pseudo-physiology which teaches that the exercise of the generative function is necessary in order to maintain one's physical and mental vigor of manhood." "... I may state that I have, after many years experience, never seen a single instant of atrophy of the generative organs from this cause.... No continent man need be deterred by this apocryphal fear of atrophy of the testes from living a chaste life."

Professor Gowers says: "With all the force that any knowledge can give, and with any authority I may have, I assert, as the result of long observation and consideration of facts of every kind, that no man ever yet was in the slightest degree or way the better for incontinence; and I am sure, further, that no man was yet anything but better for perfect continence. My warning is: Let us beware lest we give even a silent sanction to that against which I am sure we should resolutely set our face and raise our voice."

This testimony should be sufficient to satisfy anyone who has been in doubt on the subject. What is said of the man may conversely be said about the woman.

How to Banish Thoughts of Sex

When thoughts of sex enter one's atmosphere, it is useless to try to drive them away, because the thinking that is done holds them. If they do come, one should disregard them by at once thinking of one's own Thinker and Knower, and of The Realm of Permanence. Sex thoughts cannot remain in the atmosphere of such thinking.

Devotional Exercises

Those who may desire to improve themselves along the lines here indicated will find the following exercises helpful, in addition to what is shown about "breathing" in the chapter on "REGENERATION: Breathing and the Living Soul." These repetitions should be practiced regularly, at certain times, or at any time of the day:

First thing in the morning, and last thing at night:

Ever-present Consciousness! I thank Thee for Thy Presence with me this past night (or day). I ardently desire to be conscious of Thy Presence through this day (or night) and through all time. My will is to do all that I should do to become conscious of Thee and ultimately be at one with Thee.

My Judge and Knower! Guide me in all I think and do! Give me Thy Light, and the Light of Thy Knower! Let me be always conscious of Thee, that I may do all my duty and be consciously at one with Thee.

The following formula is for moral improvement and for conduct in business:

> In all that I think;
> In all that I do,
> Myself;
> My senses;
> Be honest! Be true!

As an example of a formula to have physical well-being, the following may be taken:

Every atom in my body, thrill with life to make me well. Every molecule within me, carry health from cell to cell. Cells and organs in all systems build for lasting strength and youth, Work in harmony together by the Conscious Light, as Truth.

OTHER EXERCISES

On retiring at night one may review the occurrences of the day. Judge each action according to rightness and reason concerning everything that has been done or said. Approve what has been right and condemn what has been wrong. State what should have been done, and determine to act correctly in the future. Conscience will be your guide. Then let one feel a gentle warmth and good cheer throughout the body. Charge the breath-form to guard the body throughout the night, and to awake if any undesirable influence should approach.

In order that the body may be brought into coordination with nature and under control of one's thinking, let one understand that there is a constant magnetic-electric action throughout the earth, and that one's feet are directly affected by this action. Let one assume a comfortable posture, either standing or sitting. Feel in each big toe a pulsing or throbbing. Then without moving let the throbbing be felt in the next toe and the next, until all five toes in both feet are felt to throb simultaneously. Then let the current be felt flowing upward through the instep, then the ankles, then up the legs, and steadily to the knees and along the thighs, then up into the pelvis, and then let the current of feeling be felt along the spine, between the shoulders, the neck, and through the opening of the skull into the brain. When the brain is reached, there should in time be felt a current of life, like a fountain, flowing back and stimulating the body. This will result in a harmonious feeling of good will. This can be practiced morning and evening, or at any time or place, but morning and evening are the best.

PART V

THE HUMAN BEING
FROM ADAM TO JESUS

THE STORY OF ADAM AND EVE:
The Story of Every Human Being

The story is brief. It is as brief as the history of the universe told in the first chapter of Genesis. The Bible story is like the headlines of a newspaper story—without the story. It is high time that the essence of the story, which was not told in the Bible, be known: that is, that each human being on earth was in the distant past a sexless Adam, in "Eden." Adam's sexless body was divided into a man body and a woman body, the twain Adam and Eve. Later, because of the "sin," the sexual act, they were expelled from Eden, and they came from the interior of the earth through the "Cave of Treasures" onto the outer surface of the earth. It is necessary that men and women should know of their origin, in order that the conscious selves in their human bodies can learn of and find the way back to Eden, The Realm of Permanence.

To appreciate the meaning of the story, let it be under-stood that in the Bible the term "God" means the intelligent

135

incorporeal unit, here called the Triune Self, as Knower-Thinker-Doer; that "Eden" means The Realm of Permanence; and that "Adam" means the original pure, corporeal, sexless physical body which was the first temple of man.

In the Bible it is said: "And the Lord God (Thinker-Knower of the Triune Self) formed man of the dust of the ground, and breathed into his nostrils the breath of life; and man became a living soul." (*See*: Genesis 2, v. 7). That is to say, the incorporeal Thinker-Knower of the Triune Self "breathed" its Doer part, as desire-feeling, into the pure, corporeal, sexless Adam body, composed of balanced units, which was formed "of the dust of the ground," that is, of the units of physical matter. Then the Bible story tells that God took a "rib" from the Adam body, which "rib" by extension from Adam became an Eve body. And the Adam body was a man body and the Eve body was a woman body.

Let it be understood that "God" or the "Triune Self" is incorporeal; and that "Adam" or "Adam and Eve" were composed of the "dust of the ground," which is of the unintelligent units of nature. Therefore it should be plain that the unbalancing of the balanced units of the Adam body into the Adam body and the Eve body could not affect the one-ness of "God," the Triune Self unit. The Triune Self is a unit of three parts—an individual trinity. Therefore, the feeling part of the Doer was not actually cut off from the desire part of the Doer when it was, so to say, extended into the Eve body. As long as the Doer of the Triune Self thought of itself as desire-feeling, it was and could not be other than its desire-feeling part. But when it allowed itself to think under control of its body-mind, it was hypnotized and deluded and identified itself with the unbalanced Adam and Eve bodies instead of with its Triune Self. Then from the desire-feeling in the Adam body went its feeling into the Eve body, and the desire in the Adam made of Adam a man body, and the feeling in Eve made of Eve a woman body.

Then the Thinker-Knower (Lord God) of the Triune Self said to its Doer part, as desire in Adam and as feeling in Eve in words like as of the Bible: "You are one Doer as desire-feeling in your twain bodies. You are to rule and govern your bodies as two apparently distinct, but nevertheless inseparable bodies which are to be as one body—just as each pair of hands acts for its body. Do not let your divided body serve as the means of beguiling you into believing that you are *not* one Doer acting for one body, else your divided body cannot re-unite as one inseparable desire-feeling within one undivided body.

"Your bodies are your Adam and Eve garden in which I have placed you for a while to live in the land of Eden. You, as desire-feeling, are to be my Word, and as such you are to create and give life and form to all creatures through the air, in the waters, and on the land. Do as you will with anything in your garden (bodies). What you do in the bodies which are your garden, even so shall it be through the land of Eden; for you are to be the keeper and the gardener in the land of Eden.

"In the center of your garden bodies is the Tree of Life in your Adam body; and the Tree of Good and Evil is in your Eve body. You, desire in Adam, and you, feeling in Eve, must not for your own pleasure partake of the Tree of Good and Evil, else you will leave the land of Eden and your bodies must thereafter die."

Then the Thinker-Knower (Lord God) of the Triune Self said to its Doer part, desire-feeling in the Adam and Eve bodies: "Your original undivided Adam body was formed on two spinal columns, which are as two trees; the front column tree and the back tree or column. The lower part of the front column, below what is now the sternum, was taken from the Adam two-columned body to make the Eve body. The front column, the nature Tree of Good and Evil, is for the forms of all living things which are, or which may be. The back column, the Tree of Life, is for Eternal Life in Eden, when you, the Doer as desire-feeling, will then be inseparably joined. To be inseparably joined, it was necessary that your sexless Adam body be temporarily divided into an active-passive Adam body and a passive-active Eve body, as male and female, so that the bodies could serve as scales in which your active desire and your passive feeling could be weighed and adjusted in balanced union. When you are balanced you will not be active-passive or passive-active—you will be joined in perfectly balanced equilibrium, and will be the model and pattern for nature. The balancing is to be done by your right thinking in union, that is, by the thinking of desire in your male Adam body and the thinking of feeling in your female Eve body, balanced in right relation to each other as one; and your twain bodies are the scales for the balancing. The right thinking for the balancing is for you, desire-feeling, while in your Adam and Eve bodies, to think in unison as being indivisible desire-feeling, irrespective of the divided physical body. The wrong way of thinking is for you, as desire-feeling, to think of yourself as two beings, as a desire-man-body, and as a feeling-woman-body, to be sexually related to each other."

Then the Thinker-Knower (Lord God) of the Triune Self said to its Doer, desire-feeling (the Word): "You have a desire-mind and a feeling-mind and a body-mind. You with your desire-mind and feeling-mind are to think together as of one mind, and independently of your body-mind. Your body-mind is to be used by you for the control of nature, equally balanced through the four senses. If you think together as one governing desire-feeling, your body-mind can have no power over you. Your body-mind will then be your obedient servant, for your control of nature by its thinking through the senses. But if you harken to the body-mind, which can think only through the senses for nature, then you will be self-hypnotized and will partake of the Tree of Knowledge of Good and Evil; you will be guilty of the thought of sex, and, later, of the act of sex, sin, the penalty of which is death."

Then the Thinker-Knower (Lord God) withdrew, so that its Doer, as desire-feeling in the Adam and Eve bodies, could be tested and weighed in the two bodies which served as scales, for the balancing of nature by the body-mind, and so to determine whether desire-feeling would control the body-mind and the senses, or whether the body-mind and senses would control desire-feeling.

Notwithstanding this warning, the thinking of the body-mind through the senses caused desire in the man body of Adam to look at and to think of its feeling, expressed through the woman body as Eve; and caused feeling in the Eve body to look at and to think of its desire, expressed through the man body of Adam. While desire-feeling thought as itself, without considering the relation to its bodies, each was the other in and as itself, undivided; but while desire-feeling looked at and thought of the man and woman bodies, the body-mind caused desire-feeling to think of itself as of two sexual bodies.

In many—those that subsequently became human beings—thinking of the body-mind through the senses prevailed over the thinking of desire-feeling as itself. The thinking of desire-feeling was thus deceived, deluded and separated by the sexes of the bodies. Then desire-feeling was conscious of guilt, of wrong, and was conscience-stricken. As desire and feeling they lost clear sight, and their hearing was dulled.

Then the Thinker-Knower (Lord God) of the Triune Self spoke to its Doer, desire-feeling, through the hearts of Adam and Eve, and said: "O, my Doer! I made known to you as rightful Governor of yourself and of your body that as desire-feeling it was your duty while in the Adam and Eve bodies to qualify as Governor in the land of Eden by thinking of the one-ness of desire-feeling in union, as yourself. By so thinking and doing you would be the tried and proven true Governor of yourself and would have reunited the Adam and Eve twain bodies as a balanced and immortal perfect physical body to be one of the governors in the Realm of Eden. But you have submitted yourself in thinking to be guided and controlled by the body-mind for nature through the senses, as man and as woman. Thereby you have put yourself in bondage and servitude to unbalanced nature, to leave the Realm of Eden and to be in the human world of life and death; to pass through and suffer death, and again and again to live and to die, until you learn and at last do what you should at first have done. Then the penalty of your sin will have been expiated; you will have atoned, redeemed yourself from sexual life as sin, and thereby abolished death.

"O, my Doer! I will not forsake you. Though you are a part of me, I cannot do for you what you alone must do and be responsible for as yourself, as my Doer. I will guide and guard you in so far as you will that I should guide you. I told you that which you should do, and that which you should not do. You are to choose what you will do, and then do that; and to know what you should not do, and not do that. In the human world you must abide the consequences of your choice made in Eden. You must learn to be responsible for your own thoughts and acts. As Doer of desire-feeling, your desire lives in the Adam body and your feeling lives in the Eve body. When your bodies die in the man and woman world, you will not again live in two separate bodies at the same time. You will be together in a man body or in a woman body. As desire-feeling you will enter and live in a male body, or as feeling-desire in a female body. You have made yourself the servant of your body-mind. Your body-mind cannot think of you or for you, as desire-feeling or as feeling-desire, as you really are; your body-mind can think of you only as a man body or as a woman body of unbalanced sexual nature. As desire-feeling in a man body, your desire will be expressed and your feeling will be suppressed. In a woman body your feeling will be expressed and your desire will be suppressed. Therefore in a man body your suppressed feeling will seek union with its feeling side which is expressed in the body of a woman. In a woman body your suppressed desire side will seek union with the desire expressed in the body of a man. But never can you have union of yourself as feeling-desire by sexual union of bodies. Union of bodies tantalizes and tortures and prevents desire-feeling from union with and in itself, within the one body in which it then is. The only way by which union can be brought about and realized will be for you as Doer to think together as of one mind in the man body or the woman body in which you then are—to be not as one and the other, but to think only as one. Eventually, when you in some one life, as desire-feeling in a man or as feeling-desire in a woman, refuse to think of sex and will think as one only, by so thinking the body will be regenerated and transformed to become and be a perfect sexless physical body in which you, as desire-feeling, will return to Eden and be again consciously at one with me (Lord God), Knower-Thinker-Doer, as one Triune Self complete, in The Realm of Permanence."

To repeat: The foregoing is an adaptation of Biblical language to describe in a similar manner events that took ages of earth time to transpire.

Here follows the talk of God with Adam and Eve after their departure from Eden, as recorded in *"The Forgotten Books of Eden,"* as evidence of the truth of the admonition of God to Adam and Eve in the Garden of Eden, recorded in the Bible (King James' version); and the additional evidence, in corroboration and furtherance of the colloquy between God and Adam and Eve.

"The Forgotten Books of Eden and The Lost Books of the Bible" are published in one volume by The World Publishing Company of Cleveland and New York. They gave permission to THE WORD Publishing Company of New York for the extracts published in the book *Thinking and Destiny* which are in part here repeated.

The Adam and Eve Story, After Leaving Eden, Also Called The Conflict of Adam and Eve

"This is the most ancient story in the world—it has survived because it embodies the basic fact of human life. A fact that has not changed one iota. Amid all the superficial changes of civilization's vivid array, this fact remains: the conflict of Good and Evil; the fight between Man and the Devil; the eternal struggle of human nature against sin."

"The version which we give here is the work of unknown Egyptians (the lack of historical allusion makes it impossible to date the writing)."

One critic has said of this writing:

"This is, we believe, the greatest literary discovery that the world has known."

"In general, this account begins where the Genesis story of Adam and Eve leaves off. Thus the two cannot well be compared; here we have a new chapter—a sort of sequel to the other."

"The plan of Book I is as follows:

"The careers of Adam and Eve, from the day they left Eden; their dwelling in the Cave of Treasures; their trials and temptations; Satan's manifold apparitions to them. The birth of Cain, of Abel, and of their twin sisters; Cain's love for his own twin sister, Luluwa, whom Adam and Eve wished to join to Abel; the details of Cain's murder of his brother; and Adam's sorrow and death."

It will be well to allow Adam and Eve to speak for themselves and God's voice to them:

(Chapter V, v. 4, 5) Eve speaks: "O God, forgive me my sin, the sin which I committed, and remember it not against me. For I alone caused Thy servant to fall from the garden into this lost estate, from light into this darkness, and from the abode of joy into this prison." (v. 9 to 12) Eve continues: "For Thou, O God, didst cause a slumber to come upon him, and didst take a bone from his side, and didst restore the flesh in the place of it, by Thy divine power. And Thou didst take me, the bone, and make me a woman, bright like him, with heart, reason, and speech; and in flesh, like unto his own; and Thou didst make me after the likeness of his countenance, by Thy mercy and power. O Lord, I and he are one, and Thou, O God, art our Creator, Thou are He who made us both in one day. Therefore, O God, give him life, that he may be with me in this strange land, while we dwell in it on account of our transgression."

(Chapter VI, v. 3, 4) "He, therefore, sent His Word unto them, that they should stand and be raised forthwith. And the Lord said unto Adam and Eve, 'You transgressed of your own free will, until you came out of the garden in which I had placed you.'"

(Chapter VII, v. 2) "Then God had pity on them, and said: 'O Adam, I have made My covenant with thee, and I will not turn from it; neither will I let thee return to the garden, until My covenant of the great five days and a half is fulfilled.'"

(Chapter VIII, v. 2) "Then God the Lord said unto Adam, 'When thou wast under subjection to Me, thou hadst a bright nature within thee, and for that reason couldst thou see things afar off. But after thy transgression thy bright nature was withdrawn from thee; and it was not left to thee to see things afar off, but only near at hand, after the ability of the flesh, for it is brutish.'"

(Chapter XI, v. 9, 11) And Adam said: "Remember, O Eve, the garden-land, and the brightness thereof! Whereas no sooner did we come into this Cave of Treasures than darkness compassed us round about, until we can no longer see each other."

(Chapter XVI, v. 3, 6) "Then Adam began to come out of the cave. And when he came to the mouth of it, and stood and turned his face towards the east, and saw the sun rise in glowing rays, and felt the heat thereof on his body; he was afraid of it, and thought in his heart that this flame came forth to plague him. For he thought the sun was God. (v. 10, 11, 12) But while he was thus thinking in his heart, the Word of God came unto him and said: 'O Adam, arise and stand up. This sun is not God; but it has been created to give light by day, of which I spake unto thee in the cave, saying that the dawn would break forth, and there would be light by day. But I am God who comforted thee in the night.'"

(Chapter XXV, v. 3, 4) "But Adam said unto God, 'It was in my mind to put an end to myself at once, for having transgressed Thy commandments, and for having come out of the beautiful garden; and for the bright light of which Thou hast deprived me. Yet of Thy goodness, O God, do not away with me altogether; but be favorable to me every time I die, and bring me to life.'"

(Chapter XXVI, v. 9, 11, 12) "Then came the Word of God to Adam and said unto him, 'Adam, as for the sun, if I were to take it and bring it to thee, days, hours, years and months would all come to naught, and the covenant I have made with thee would never be fulfilled. Yea, rather, bear long and calm thy soul while thou abidest night and day; until the fulfillment of the days, and the time of My covenant is come. Then shall I come and save thee, O Adam, for I do not wish that thou be afflicted.'"

(Chapter XXXVIII, v. 1, 2) "After these things the Word of God came to Adam, and said unto him: 'O Adam, as to the fruit of the Tree of Life, for which thou askest, I will not give it thee now, but when the 5500 years are fulfilled. Then will I give thee of the fruit of the Tree of Life, and thou shall eat, and live for ever—thou and Eve.'"

(Chapter XLI, v. 9, 10, 12) "Adam began to pray with his voice before God, and said: 'O Lord, when I was in the garden and saw the water that flowed from under the Tree of Life, my heart did not desire, neither did my body require to drink of it; neither did I know thirst, for I was living; and above that which I am now. But now, O God, I am dead; my flesh is parched with thirst. Give me of the Water of Life that I may drink of it and live.'"

(Chapter XLII, v. 1 to 4) "Then came the Word of God to Adam and said unto him: 'O Adam, as to what thou sayest, "Bring me into a land where there is rest," it is not another land than this, but it is the kingdom of heaven where alone there is rest. But thou canst not make thy entrance into it at present, but only after thy judgment is past and fulfilled. Then will I make thee go up into the kingdom of heaven.'"

What in these pages is written about the "Realm of Permanence" may have been thought of as "Paradise" or the "Garden of Eden." When each Doer of its Triune Self was with its Thinker and Knower in The Realm of Permanence, it had to undergo the trial to balance feeling-and-desire, in the course of which trial it was temporarily in a dual body, the "twain," by the separation of its perfect body into a male body for its desire side, and a female body for its feeling side. The Doers in all human bodies gave way to the temptation by the body-mind for sex, whereupon they were exiled from The Realm of Permanence to re-exist on the crust of the earth in man bodies or in woman bodies. Adam and Eve were one Doer divided into a male body and a female body. When the two bodies died, the Doer did not thereafter re-exist in two bodies, but as desire-and-feeling in a male body, or as feeling-and-desire in a female body. All Doers in human bodies will continue to re-exist on this earth until, by their own efforts, by thinking, they find The Way, and return to The Realm of Permanence. The story of Adam and Eve is the story of each human on this earth.

Thus can be epitomized into a few words the stories of the "Garden of Eden," of "Adam and Eve," and of the "fall of man"; or, in the words of this book, The "Realm of Permanence," the story of "feeling-and-desire," and that of the "descent of the Doer" into this temporal human world. The teaching of the inner life, by Jesus, is the teaching of the Doer's return to The Realm of Permanence.

That the Bible story of Adam and Eve is the story of every human being is clearly and unequivocally stated in the New Testament, as follows:

"Wherefore, as by one man sin entered into the world, and death by sin; and so death passed upon all men, for that all have sinned." Romans 5, v. 12.

From Adam to Jesus

It is well to repeat: The story of Adam is the story of the conscious self in every human being that has existed or now exists on this earth. Each one was originally an Adam, and subsequently an Adam and Eve, in the "Garden of Eden" (The Realm of Permanence). Because of the "original sin," they came into this man and woman world of birth and death. Here, in this world, through all the lives that are necessary, the conscious self in each human body must learn of its origin, and of the futility of human life as desire-feeling in the man body or as feeling-desire in the woman body.

"In the beginning" in Genesis refers to the Adam body in the land of Eden, and it also relates to the prenatal preparation of the human body for the return of the conscious self as desire-feeling in each of its re-existences in the human world, until its final "incarnation" as a "Jesus"—to redeem the human by balancing its feeling-and-desire into inseparable union. So it will transform the human body into a perfect sexless immortal physical body in which the *Son*, the Doer, returns to his *Father in heaven* (Thinker-Knower), as a complete Triune Self in The Realm of Permanence.

About two thousand years ago Jesus, as desire-feeling in a human body, came to tell human beings about their individual conscious selves and about each one's Father in heaven; and how to change and transform their bodies. He explained and demonstrated how to do this by doing it himself.

148

In Matthew, the first of the four Gospels, the connections of the lives between Adam and Jesus from David onward are stated in the first Chapter, from the 1st to the 18th verses. It is also important to bear in mind that the relation is borne out by the argument made by Paul in his 15th Chapter of 1st Corinthians, verses 19 to 22: "If in this life only we have hope in Christ, we are of all men the most miserable. But now is Christ risen from the dead, and become the first fruits of them that slept. For since by man came death, by man came also the resurrection of the dead. For as in Adam all die, even so in Christ shall all be made alive."

This shows that every human body must die because it is a sexual body. The "original sin" is the sexual act, as the result of which every human body is molded in the form of sex and is born through sex. And because feeling-and-desire as the conscious self in the body is made to think of itself as the sex of its body, it repeats the act. It cannot think of itself as a conscious immortal self which cannot die. But when it understands the situation it is in—that it is hidden or lost in the coils of flesh and blood in which it is—and when it can think of itself as the conscious Doer part of its Father in heaven, its own Triune Self, it will eventually overcome and conquer sexuality. Then it removes the sign—the mark of the beast, the sex mark—which is the mark of death. There is then no death, because the thinking of the conscious Doer as feeling-and-desire will have regenerated and thereby transformed the human mortal into an immortal physical body. Paul explains this in verses 47 to 50: "The first man is of the earth, earthy; the second man is the Lord from heaven. As is the earthy, such are they also that are earthy; and as is the heavenly, such are they also that are heavenly. And as we have borne the image of the earthy we shall also bear the image of the heavenly. Now this I say, brethren, that flesh and blood cannot inherit the kingdom of God; neither doth corruption inherit incorruption."

The difference between the first man as of the earthy and the second man as the Lord from heaven is that the first man, Adam, became the earthy sexual human Adam body. Whereas the second man means that the conscious self, feeling-and-desire, in the human earthly flesh and blood body has regenerated and transformed the human sexual body into a perfect sexless immortal heavenly body, which is the "Lord from heaven."

The more complete and direct line of descent from father to son is given by Luke in Chapter 3, beginning at verse 23: "And Jesus himself began to be about 30 years of age, being (as was supposed) the son of Joseph, which was the son of Heli," and concluding in verse 38: "Which was the son of Enos, which was the son of Seth, which was the son of Adam, which was the son of God." There the time and connective order of lives from the life of Adam to the life of Jesus are recorded. The important point of the record is that it relates the life of Adam with the life of Jesus.

Matthew thus gives the genealogy from David to Jesus. And Luke shows the direct line of sonship—back through Adam—"which was the son of God."

Concerning mankind, the foregoing means that desire-feeling, called Jesus, entered a human body of this world, similarly as desire-feeling re-exists in all human bodies. But Jesus as desire-feeling came not as the ordinary re-existence. Jesus came to save from death not only the human body which he took on. Jesus came into the human world at the certain cycle of time to inaugurate and proclaim his message, and for a particular purpose. His message was to tell the desire-feeling or feeling-desire in the human that it has a "Father" in heaven; that it is asleep and dreaming in the human body; that it should awake from its dream of human life and know itself, as itself, in the human body; and then, it should regenerate and transform the human body into a perfect sexless immortal physical body, and return to its Father in heaven.

That is the message that Jesus brought to mankind. His particular purpose in coming was to prove to mankind by his personal example how to conquer death.

This can be done by psychological, physiological, and biological processes. The psychological is by thinking. The physiological is by means of the quadrigemina, the red nucleus, and the pituitary body through the breath-form, the "living soul," which automatically controls and coordinates all movements through the involuntary nervous system of the body. The biological process is worked out by the procreative organs of the man and woman bodies in the production of spermatozoa and the ova. Each male or female germ cell must divide twice before the male sperm can enter the female ovum for the reproduction of a human body.

But what keeps these physiological and biological processes of the ages of mankind in operation? The answer is: Thinking! Thinking according to the Adam type and the Eve type causes the reproduction of male and female bodies. Why, and how?

Man and woman think as they do because they do not understand how to think otherwise, and because they are urged by their sexual organs and the germ cells developed in the generative system of each to unite with a body of the opposite sex.

The physical process is: The sex-urge in the generative system of the human acts through the blood and nerves on the breath-form in the front part of the pituitary body, which acts on the red nucleus, which acts on the quadrigemina, which react on the sex organs of the body, which prompt the body-mind in the breath-form to think of the relation of its sex to its opposite sex. Unless there is the predetermined will for self-control, the sex impulse is almost overpowering. The psychological process is then carried on by the thinking of the body-mind, which writes the plan of action on the breath-form, and the breath-form automatically causes the physical actions as determined by the thinking to perform the sexual act in the manner desired.

The story of the sin of Adam being the story of the conscious Doer in every human being, and the passage through human life from Adam to Jesus, are told in the New Testament in Romans 6, v. 23, as follows: "For the wages of sin is Death; but the gift of God is eternal life through Jesus Christ our Lord."

The individual human who desires to conquer death should banish all thought of sexuality by distinct thinking and willing to have a sexless physical body. There should be no instruction as to how the body is to be changed. The definite thinking will be inscribed on the breath-form. The breath-form will in due time automatically regenerate and transform the human body to be a perfect sexless physical body of immortal youth.

Jesus, the "Forerunner" for "Conscious Immortality"

Among other things the Gospels have this to say about the generation of Jesus and his appearance as a human being:

Matthew Chapter 1, v. 18: "Now the birth of Jesus Christ was on this wise: When as his mother Mary was espoused to Joseph, before they came together, she was found with child of the Holy Ghost. (19) Then Joseph her husband, being a just man, and not willing to make her a publick example, was minded to put her away privily. (20) But while he thought on these things, behold, the angel of the Lord appeared unto him in a dream, saying, Joseph, thou son of David, fear not to take unto thee Mary thy wife: for that which is conceived in her is of the Holy Ghost. (21) And she shall bring forth a son, and thou shalt call his name JESUS: for he shall save his people from their sins. (23) Behold a virgin shall be with child, and shall bring forth a son, and they shall call his name Emmanuel, which being interpreted is, God with us. (25) And (Joseph) knew her not till she had brought forth her first-born son; and he called his name JESUS."

Luke Chapter 2 v. 46: "And it came to pass, that after three days they found him in the temple, sitting in the midst of the doctors, both hearing them, and asking questions. (47) And all that heard him were astonished at his understanding and answers. (48) And when they saw him they were amazed; and his mother said unto him, Son, why hast thou thus dealt with us? behold, thy father and I have sought thee sorrowing. (49) And he said unto them, How is it that ye sought me? wist ye not that I must be about my Father's business? (50) And they understood him not the saying which he spake unto them. (52) And Jesus increased in wisdom and stature, and in favour with God and man."

Chapter 3, v. 21 "Now when all the people were baptized, it came to pass, that Jesus, also being baptized, and praying, the heaven was opened. (22) And the Holy Ghost descended in a bodily shape like a dove upon him, and a voice came from heaven, which said, Thou art my beloved Son; in thee I am well pleased. (23) And Jesus himself began to be about thirty years of age, being (as was supposed) the son of Joseph, which was the son of Heli, (24) which was the son of Matthat, which was the son of Levi, which was the son of Melchi, which was the son of Janna, which was the son of Joseph, etc., Here follow all the verses from 25 to 38: ...which was the son of Seth, which was the son of Adam, which was the son of God."

The corporeal physical body in which Jesus lived may not have been generally known. This is made probable by the fact that it is written that Judas was paid 30 pieces of silver to identify Jesus from his disciples, by kissing him. But from various Bible passages it is evident that the term JESUS was to represent the conscious self, the Doer, or feeling-and-desire, in every human body, and *not* the body. However that may be, the incorporeal Jesus as self-conscious desire-and-feeling walked the earth in a human physical body at that time, just as at the present time every human body has in it the immortal feeling-desire conscious self in a woman body, or a self-con-scious desire-feeling in a man body. And without this self-con-scious self there is no human being.

A difference between the desire-feeling as Jesus at that time and the desire-feeling in a man body of today, is that Jesus knew himself to be the immortal Doer, the Word, desire-feeling in the body, whereas no human being knows *what* he is, awake or asleep. Further, a purpose for the coming of Jesus at that time was to tell that he was the immortal self *in* the body, and *not* the body itself. And he especially came to set an example, that is, to be a "forerunner" of what the human should do, and be, in order to find himself in the body and eventually to be able to say: "I and my Father are one." This meant that he, Jesus, being conscious of himself as the Doer in his physical body, thereby was conscious of his direct Sonship relation to his Lord, God (Thinker-and-Knower) of his Triune Self.

Nearly 2000 years have passed since Jesus walked the earth in a physical body. Since then innumerable churches have been built in his name. But his message has not been understood. Perhaps it was not intended that his message should be understood. It is one's own conscious self which must save one from death; that is, the human must become conscious of himself, as Doer while in the body—conscious of himself as distinct and different from the physical body—in order to achieve conscious immortality. With the finding of Jesus in one's body, the human being may change his physical sexual body to be a sexless body of immortal life. That this is so, is confirmed by what has been left in the Books of the New Testament.

In *"The Gospel according to St. John"* it is said:

Chapter 1, v. 1 to 5: "In the beginning was the Word, and the Word was with God, and the Word was God. The same was in the beginning with God. All things were made by him; and without him was not anything made that was made. In him was life; and the life was the light of men. And the light shineth in the darkness; and the darkness comprehended it not."

Those are enigmatic statements. They have been repeated endlessly but nobody seems to know what they mean. They mean that Jesus, the Word, desire-feeling, the Doer part of his Triune Self, was sent on a mission to the world to tell of Jesus, desire-feeling, and of "God," Thinker-Knower of that Triune Self. He, Jesus, knowing himself as distinct from his body, was the Light, but the darkness—those who were not so conscious—comprehended it not.

The important point of the mission on which he, Jesus, was sent to the world was to tell that others could also become conscious as the Doer parts of their individual Triune Selves, that is, as the "sons of each one's respective Father." That at that time there were those who understood and followed him, is shown in verse 12:

> "But as many as received him, to them gave he power to become the sons of God, even to them that believe on his name: (13) Which were born, not of blood, nor of the will of the flesh, nor of the will of man, but of God."

But nothing is heard of these in the Gospels. The Gospels were to tell the people at large, but those of the people who wanted to know more than was told publicly, sought him out, even as Nicodemus sought him out, at night; and those who sought him and wished to become sons of their individual "Gods" got the instruction which could not be given to the multitudes. In

John Chapter 16, v. 25, Jesus says: "These things have I spoken unto you in proverbs; but the time cometh, when I shall no more speak to you in proverbs, and I shall show you plainly of the Father."

This he could do only after he had sufficiently acquainted them about themselves as being the Word, which made them conscious as themselves.

The word, desire-feeling, in the human, is the beginning of all things, and without it the world could not be as it is. It is what the human thinks and does with his desire and feeling that will determine the destiny of mankind.

Jesus came at a crucial period in human history, when his teaching could be given and understood by some, to try to turn man's thinking from war and destruction toward a life for Conscious Immortality. In this he was a forerunner to teach, to explain, to show, and to demonstrate by personal example how to immortalize his physical body, so that, as he told those whom he left behind: Whither I am, there may ye also be.

After appearing among the doctors in the temple at the age of 12, nothing is heard of him until he appears when about 30 years old, at the river Jordan, to be baptized by John. The interim was a period of eighteen years of preparation in seclusion, during which he made ready for immortalizing his physical body. It is stated in:

Matthew, Chapter 3, v. 16: "And Jesus, when he was baptized, went up straightway out of the water and, lo, the heavens were opened unto him, and he saw the Spirit of God descending like a dove, and lighting upon him (17) and a voice from heaven saying, This is my beloved Son, in whom I am well pleased."

That indicated that he was Jesus, the Christ. As Jesus, the Christ, he was one with God; that is, the Doer was united with his Thinker-Knower, his God, which definitely immortalized his physical body and dedicated him to the work as "Forerunner" and as belonging to the Order of Melchisedec, a priest of the most high God.

Hebrew 8, Chapter 7, v. 15: "And it is yet far more evident, for that after the similitude of Melchisedec there arises another priest, (16) who is made, not after the law of a carnal commandment, but after the power of an endless life. (17) For he testifieth, Thou art a priest for ever after the Order of Melchisedec. (24) But this man, because he continueth ever, has an unchangeable priesthood."

Chapter 9, v. 11: "But Christ being a high priest of good things to come, by a greater and more perfect tabernacle, not made with hands, that is to say, not of this building."

The early outposts that Jesus left behind are only landmarks that show a way to the kind of inner life that must be lived in order to know and to enter the kingdom of God. As is written, when one asked the Lord when his kingdom would come, he answered: "When two shall be one and that which is without as that which is within; and the male with the female, neither male nor female." That means that desire-and-feeling would then not be unbalanced in human bodies with desire predominating in the male bodies and feeling predominating in the female bodies, but would be blended and balanced and amalgamated in sexless, immortal, perfect physical bodies of eternal life—the second temple—each as a Doer-Thinker-Knower, a Triune Self complete, in The Realm of Permanence.

———————

Much of the unhappy past which has been the lot of humanity for nearly 2,000 years starts indirectly from the perversion of people's minds due to erroneous teachings concerning the meaning of the "trinity." A good deal of this was caused by the alterations, changes, additions, and deletions made in the original source materials. For those reasons, Bible passages cannot be depended upon as being unaltered and according to original sources. Many of the changes centered around attempts to explain the "trinity" as being three persons in one, as one Universal God—however, only for those who belonged to a given denomination. Some people will in time realize that there can be no one universal God, but that there is the individual God that speaks within human beings—as each one can testify who will listen to the Thinker-Knower of his Triune Self speaking in his own heart as his conscience. That will be better understood when the human learns how to consult his "conscience" habitually. He may then realize that he is the Doer part of his Triune Self—as indicated in these pages and, in more detail, in the book *Thinking and Destiny*.

———————

Let the reader realize that the immortalized body of Jesus was beyond the possibility of physical suffering, and that, as Doer-Thinker-Knower of his individual Triune Self complete, he entered a state of Bliss quite beyond the conception of any human imagining.

Such is also the reader's ultimate destiny, for soon or late he must, and finally will, choose to take the first step on The Great Way to Conscious Immortality.

The Twelve States Of The Re-existing Doer
From One Life To The Next Life

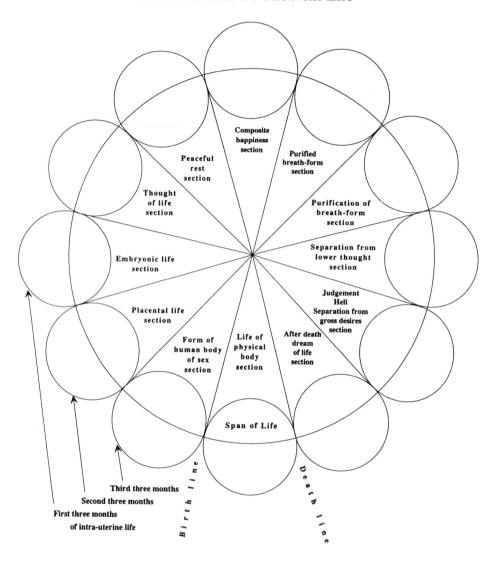

Composite happiness section

Peaceful rest section

Purified breath-form section

Thought of life section

Purification of breath-form section

Embryonic life section

Separation from lower thought section

Placental life section

Judgement Hell Separation from gross desires section

Form of human body of sex section

Life of physical body section

After death dream of life section

Span of Life

Third three months

Second three months

First three months of intra-uterine life

Birth line

Death line

Section of the Human Brain
in the Median Line

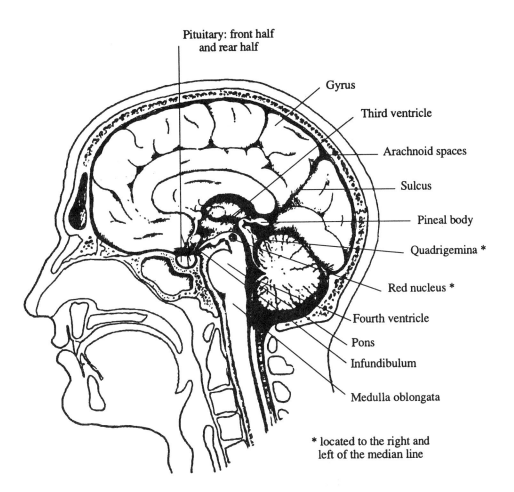

Pituitary: front half
and rear half

Gyrus

Third ventricle

Arachnoid spaces

Sulcus

Pineal body

Quadrigemina *

Red nucleus *

Fourth ventricle

Pons

Infundibulum

Medulla oblongata

* located to the right and
left of the median line

INDEX

A

ADAM AND EVE. Story of — 34, 81, 125, 135-147, 148; — is the story of every human being, 81, 147, 148, 152; Essence of —, not told in the Bible, 135; The story of — after leaving Eden, 141, 144; Colloquy between God and — 141.

AIA UNIT, 32, 33.

B

BABY, THE — 7-10, 50-51, 53.

BIBLE." "The Lost Books of the — 141.

BIRTH/DEATH, 6, 22, 34, 47, 69, 80, 88, 148.

BODY, The human — 7, 33, 54, 80, 82, 99, 115, 120, 149; — a machine, 7, 8, 9, 14, 38-40; — a model for nature, 7, 39, 77, 81.

BOY AND GIRL, Attraction between — 4.

BREATH, or Breathing, The — 40-41, 100, 105-108, 115-116; Feeling where the — goes, 106-107, 116-117.

BREATH-FORM, or "Living Soul," The — 32, 34, 38-41, 43, 59, 77, 78, 79, 83, 85, 93-94, 99-100, 102, 103, 107-109, 112, 116, 120, 151-152. *See* Pituitary body.

C

CHILD, The — 37-62; "Mother, where did I come from?" 9, 48, 52; Its questions, and the answers, 2, 3, 9, 10, 11, 17, 47-49, 52-54, 58-62; The results, 60. *See also* Education of — Real — 2, 50-62; World of make believe, 14, 15, 16, 20, 21.

CIVILIZATION(S), 28, 30, 37, 44, 61, 124; — of U.S., 28.

CONCEPTION, Human — 33, 39.

CONSCIENCE, 105, 132, 159.

CONSCIOUS *of* or *as*, 31, 34, 45, 46, 48, 55, 77, 86, 112.

CONSCIOUS LIGHT, 3, 68, 78, 79, 81, 83, 84, 86, 88, 91, 95, 96, 110, 120, 125, 132; in nature, 8, 78, 83, 84, 110.

CONSCIOUS SELF, The, 2, 28, 40, 56, 80-88, 89, 93, 103, 148; — is *not* the body, 2, 45, 63, 89, 94; Entrance of — into the body, 4, 9, 21-22, 51, 89; Functioning of — in the brain, 95, 96, 110, 111. *See also* Pituitary body; Finding and freeing of — 56, 80, 81, 84-88, 90, 111, 127.

CONSCIOUSNESS ABSOLUTE, 31.

CONTINENCE, 128, 103-104

D

DEATH, 5, 22, 100, 140, 149; Saving from — 80, 102-108, 149; Victory over — 103, 116, 125; After-death states, 3, 27, 32, 33, 41, 43, 103, 120.

DE-HYPNOTIZATION, Self — 86, 89-98.

DESIRE(S), 41, 42, 64, 65, 67, 70, 73, 79, 86, 87, 121 — for sex, 67, 80, 85, 87, 116; — for self-knowledge, 67-69, 80; Four classes of — 68-69, 87.

DESIRE AND FEELING, in the "Adam"-body, 33, 126, 135-137, 138, 139, 148; Isolation of — 45, 76, 86, 94. *See also* Doer in the body.

DOER, in the body, The — 31, 38, 41, 48, 120; When it enters the body, 9, 22, 27, 50, 90; The re-existing — 33, 40, 75, 80, 122 147, 150. *See* Pituitary body.

DOER, The — part, of the Triune Self, 22, 31, 33, 41, 46, 51, 54, 55, 60, 63, 67, 70, 72, 76, 78, 99, 102, 112, 113, 114, 126, 136, 137, 138, 147, 148, 149, 155-156, 159; Self-exiled, 33, 35, 62; Separation into male and female, 64, 65, 67, 71, 73, 126, 146. *See* Story of Adam and Eve.

DREAMS, The senses in — 96; — in dreamless sleep, 96.

162

E

EDEN." The "Garden of — 33, 63, 99, 126, 141, 148; The "Forgotten Books of — 141.

EDUCATION, Real — of the child, 2, 47, 49, 50-62.

ELEMENTS, Primordial — 31.

ETERNAL, Living in the — 35, 98, 106.

EXERCISES, Devotional — 131.

EXPEDIENCY, 105.

F

FEELING, 41, 42, 45, 46, 56, 61, 63-76, 79, 84, 86, 92, 93, 97, 98, 107, 112, 136, 137, 139, 140, 158, — is *not* a "fifth" sense, 50, 94.

"FORERUNNER," The — 7, 153-159.

FREEDOM, 84, 88, 92, 104, 110, 118.

FREEMASONRY, 63.

G

GERM CELLS, 7, 85, 101, 102, 108, 116, 151.

GESTATION, Human — 10, 40, 99.

H

HISTORY, Prehistoric — 33, 35, 63.

HYPNOSIS, Self-, 66, 67, 89.

I

"I," IN THE BODY, The — 9, 10, 43, 44, 89, 90, 93. *See* Conscious self; Doer.

IDENTITY, of the human, The, "self" in the body, 21, 22; engulfed by the senses, 15, 21, 57. *See* "Conscious self."

ILLUMINATION, 86.

IMMORTALITY, Conscious — 102, 103, 105, 155, 157, 159.

INITIATIONS, 101.

INSPIRATION, Moments of — 21.

INTELLIGENCE, in nature, 8, 79, 83, 96, 110.

"ISOLATION," of feeling; — of desire, 45, 46, 56, 76, 84, 86, 92.

J

"JESUS," Genealogy from Adam to — 148-152; — as desire/ feeling, 148, 150; — in a physical body, 155; Message of — 150-151; Mission of — 156; the "Forerunner," 148-152, 155, 157.

K

KINGDOM OF GOD, — when to come, 127, 158.

KINGDOM OF HEAVEN, 5, 146.

"KNOW THYSELF," 77-88.

L

LIFE, Four periods of — 1-4; What is —? 123.

LOVE, 76, 115; True — 88.

M

MATTER, Definition of — 111.

MELCHISEDEC, The Order of — 157.

MEMORY, Human, 30, 100; Sense — 20, 22, 30, 100, 112; — of the self, 30, 59.

MENTAL ATTITUDE, 26, 104.

METABOLISM, anabolism, catabolism, 100.

MIND, THE BODY — 46, 55, 91-92, 105; Control of the — 46, 56, 73, 84, 92, 96, 97, 109, 113. *See* Pituitary body.

MIND, THE DESIRE —, 46, 56, 92; Training of — 56, 61.

MIND, THE FEELING —, 46, 56, 92; Training of — 56, 61.

MINDS, The three — 46, 55, 59, 91, 94, 111.

MYSTERIES, The — 101.

N

NATURE. Conscious Light in — 8, 78, 83, 84, 110; Intelligence in — 78, 83, 109; — units, 31, 32, 34 70, 77, 83, 112, 121, 136.

NERVOUS SYSTEM. The — Voluntary, cerebro-spinal, —, 41, 57, 69, 75, 79, 82, 109, 120, 151; Involuntary, sympathetic — 57, 69, 74, 82, 110, 120. *See* Pituitary body.

O

ORDER OF PROGRESSION, The Eternal — 30, 52, 84, 109, 116.

P

PARADISE, 33, 34, 63, 99, 146. See Realm of Permanence.

PARTITION OF FORGETFULNESS, The — 19, 24, 25, 27, 56.

PERFECT BODY, The — sexless, immortal, physical body, 63, 66, 69, 85, 100-101, 114, 152; Ancient division of — into male and female, 73; Anatomy of — 69-70, 81, 82, and changes in the — 71, 74, 75; Functional activities of the — 81, 82. See Temple, Twain.

PERFECTION, 35, 110.

PINEAL BODY, The — 78, 83, 95, 111.

PITUITARY BODY, 32, 78, 95, 109; Its location and functions, 95, 97, 109; The breath-form (living soul) in the — 32, 109; Nature government in the front part of — 83, 93, 97, 109, 120; Doer government in the rear part of the — 32, 83, 93, 97, 109, 111, 120; How the Doer connects with the breath-form — 93, 111.

PROTECTION, by one's Thinker and Knower, 104.

PSYCHOLOGY, 32, 37.

PURPOSE OF THIS BOOK, The — 35.

R

REALM OF PERMANENCE, The — 5, 33, 35, 52, 63, 69, 80, 99, 100, 101, 102, 104, 113, 114, 115, 116, 117, 127, 135, 141, 146, 147, 148, 158.

RED NUCLEUS, The — 82, 11, 151.

RE-EXISTENCE, 22, 40, 75, 148, 150.

REGENERATION, 1, 84, 85, 99, 101, 102, 113, 150, 151; Breathing, feeling and thinking in — 99-113; Purpose of — 150-151.

RIB OF ADAM, 64, 81, 126, 136.

S

SELF-KNOWLEDGE, 83, 86-88; Steps to — 44, 45, 47, 89-98.

SENSATIONS, 56, 67, 73, 120, 121.

SENSE(S). The four — 30, 32, 50, 55, 68-70, 78; — knowledge, 83, 109; — in dream, 96.

SEX, — attraction, 42; Desire for — 67, 68, 80, 87, 116; Indulgence in — 85; Thoughts of — 85, 108, 130.

SEXUALITY, 101, 103, 104, 110, 125, 149, 152.

"SIN," The original — 34, 67, 80, 99, 125 148, 149. See Adam and Eve.

SOUL. The —; "Living soul," The — 32, 38, 41, 47, 94, 99, 136, 151. See also Breath-form; Pituitary body.

T

TEMPLE, The first — 33, 63, 69, 81, 136; The second — 35, 52, 158.

THINKING, The — of boy and girl, 20, 26, 27; The — of man and woman, 26, 27; Four stages in — 91; — according to type, 151

TREE of Good and Evil, 126.

TREE of Life, 110, 137.

TRINITY. THE INDIVIDUAL — 22, 33, 136, 158. See Triune Self.

TRIUNE SELF, The —; The three parts of — 33; The Doer, 33; The Knower/Thinker of — 33.

TWAIN, The immortal —, the Doer, feeling-and-desire, 63-76; Trial and test of —, 63-66, 146-147.

U

UNIT(S), A, 31, 39, 45, 112; Nature — 31, 32, 34, 70, 77, 83, 112, 121, 136; Intelligent— 31, 34, 112; The aia — 32, 33; The breath-form — 32, 34, 39-41, 58, 99-100; Sense — 31, 32, 34; Progression of — 74; Balancing of — 116, 127.

W

"WHO AM I?", 10, 48, 51, 58, 61.

WORD, The — 144, 145, 146; — Desire/feeling, 137, 138.

WORLD of make-believe, 14, 15, 16, 20, 21; of boy and girl, 14, 19, 27; of man and woman, 19, 27.

AFTERWORD

After having read *MAN AND WOMAN AND CHILD*, you undoubtedly will want to seek more information from the same source in *THINKING AND DESTINY*. You are therefore invited to inquire about a special offer. Write to:

The Word Foundation, Inc.
P.O. Box 17510
Rochester, NY 14617
www.thewordfoundation.org

The succeeding pages tell, in part, what *THINKING AND DESTINY* contains and what it can do for you.

THINKING AND DESTINY

by Harold Waldwin Percival

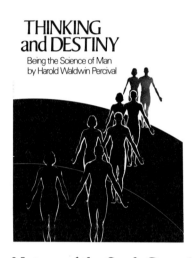

1021 pages of text and foreword, including 30 pages of symbols, illustrations and charts, 31 pages of definitions and explanations, and an 11-page comprehensive index.

No single work reveals so clearly and so much on Man, his origin, progression, and ultimate destiny. This unique book...

... **Explains the Purpose** of life; What and where you are; Nature of the Soul; Consciousness; What happens at and after death.

... **Tells how thoughts** are created and exteriorized as objects, acts, and events in the lives of individuals and collectively.

... **Discloses how you** alone control your life by your thinking, which not only can change your Destiny but your body, too.

... **Teaches the steps** that you and everyone must sooner or later take on the Great Way of Regeneration and Redemption.

Partial List of Subjects from the Table of Contents

PURPOSE AND PLAN OF THE UNIVERSE

Theories about the Soul. An accident is part of a thought. The wrath of God. Innate faith in justice. Story of Original Sin.

OPERATION OF THE LAW OF THOUGHT AS DESTINY

A thought is a being. How thoughts are created. Physical, psychic, mental, and noetic results of thoughts. Power of a thought. Hastening or delaying destiny. Responsibility. Conscience. Sin.

PHYSICAL DESTINY

Circumstances at birth. Healthy or sickly bodies. Unjust persecutions. Errors of justice. Span of life. Manner of death. Money. Poverty. Reversals. Wealth or inheritance is no accident. Rise and fall of nations. Agents of the Law. Priests. Gods. Intelligences govern order of events.

PSYCHIC DESTINY

Prenatal influences. Conception. Inheritance of former thoughts. First years of life. Mediumship. Materializations. Seances. Clairvoyance. Psychic powers. Vibrations. Colors. Astrology. Demon alcohol. Dreams. Nightmares. Hypnosis. Process of dying. To be conscious at death. States after death. Communications with the dead. Awareness that the body has died. Judgment. Hell is made by desires. The devil. Heaven is a reality.

MENTAL DESTINY

The Triune Self. An Intelligence. Active, passive, real thinking. Morality of thinking. Sense-knowledge and self-knowledge. Honest thinking. Dishonest thinking. Responsibility

167

and duty. Intuition. Genius. Realm of Permanence. Trial test of the sexes. Fall of Man. Wise men. Cycles and rise of the latest. Our age of thought. Mysticism. Spiritism. Mental healing. Thoughts are seeds of disease. Purpose of disease. Real cure. No escape from payment. Faith. Mesmerism. Self-hypnosis. Self-suggestion.

Ancient knowledge. Eastern movement. Pranayama, its dangers. System of Pantanjali, his eight steps of yoga. Meaning of Sanscrit. Traces of ancient teaching. What the West wants.

States of a human in deep sleep, in trance. Twelve stages between re-existences. Mental hells and heavens.

SPIRITUAL DESTINY

Self-knowledge available to humans. History of the Triune Self. The Light of the Intelligence. Intelligence in nature. Lunar germ. Divine, immaculate conception in the head. Regeneration of physical body. Hiram Abiff. Freemasonry. Origin of Christianity. Free will and destiny.

RE-EXISTENCE

Death of the body. The doer after death. Doer in Realm of Permanence. Fall of the doer. Story of feeling-and-desire. Spell of the sexes. Purpose of re-existence. Error of "I".

After death. Doer portion readies to re-exist. Thoughts summarized at death. Events determined at death for next life. Your family, sex. Changing sex. Time between re-existences. Memory after death. Why we do not remember previous re-existences. When re-existences stop. A lost soul. Hells inside earth. Lechers. Drunkards. Drug fiends. State of a lost doer.

GODS AND THEIR RELIGIONS

On what religions are based. Belief in a personal God. Classes of Gods. Creation of Gods. Gods of Christians. Qualities of a

God. A God's knowledge. His objects, interests. Moral codes. Flattery. How Gods lost power. What a God can and cannot do. Unbelievers. Prayer. Benefits of belief in a God. Seeking God. Outside, inner teachings. Christianity, St. Paul. Jehovah. Story of Jesus. Kingdom of God. Trinity.

THE GREAT PATH: REGENERATION

Future development. The Great Way. Brotherhoods. Initiations. Alchemists. Rosicrucians. Threefold Way. Lunar, solar, light germs. Body changes. Entering the Path. Advances on the Path. A new life opens. Perfect, immortal, sexless physical body. The Way in the earth. Traveler leaves the world. What he sees. Shades of the dead. How to enter on The Way. Honesty and truthfulness the basis.

THE POINT OR CIRCLE

Creation of a thought. Method of thinking. Thinking without creating destiny. Pre-chemistry. Dimensions. Heavenly bodies. Time, Space.

THE CIRCLE OR ZODIAC

The Twelve Nameless Points. Symbolism and value of the Zodiac. How it reveals the purpose of the Universe. As a record of history and prophecy.

THINKING: THE WAY TO CONSCIOUS IMMORTALITY

For whom this system of thinking is presented. Becoming conscious of Consciousness. Stages on The Way to Conscious Immortality.